God in the World

Karl Rahner

God in the World

A Guide to Karl Rahner's Theology

THOMAS F. O'MEARA, O.P.

A Michael Glazier Book

LITURGICAL PRESS
Collegeville, Minnesota

www.litpress.org

A Michael Glazier Book published by Liturgical Press.

Cover design by David Manahan, o.s.b.
Cover photo courtesy of istockphoto.com.

Photo on page ii courtesy of Catholic News Service.

Excerpts from the English translation of *The Roman Missal* © 1973, International Committee on English in the Liturgy, Inc. (ICEL); excerpt from the English translation of *The Liturgy of the Hours* © 1974, (ICEL). All rights reserved.

Prayer for Advent is taken from *Dominican Prayer: Morning and Evening Prayer with Daytime and Night Prayer.* Chicago: Dominicans, Province of St. Albert the Great, 1994.

Scripture quotations are from the Revised Standard Version of the Bible, Apocrypha, copyright 1957; The Third and Fourth Books of Maccabees and Psalm 151, copyright 1977 by the Division of Christian Education of the National Council of the Churches of Christ in the United States of America. Used by permission. All rights reserved.

1   2   3   4   5   6   7   8   9

Library of Congress Cataloging-in-Publication Data

O'Meara, Thomas F., 1935–
    God in the world : a guide to Karl Rahner's theology / Thomas O'Meara.
      p. cm.
    "A Michael Glazier book."
    Includes bibliographical references and index.
    ISBN-13: 978-0-8146-5222-0 (alk. paper)
    ISBN-10: 0-8146-5222-0 (alk. paper)
    1. Raher, Karl, 1904– . I. Title.

BX4705.R287O54   2007
230'.2092—dc22

                                               2006012387

Contents

Abbreviations

BR   Karl Neufeld, *Die Brüder Rahner. Eine Biographie* (Freiburg: Herder, 1994)

DKR   Andreas Batlogg et al., *Der Denkweg Karl Rahners. Quellen—Enwicklungen—Perspektiven* (Mainz: Matthias-Grünewald, 2004)

F   Karl Rahner, *Foundations of Christian Faith* (New York: Crossroad, 1978)

FW   Karl Rahner, *Faith in a Wintry Season* (New York: Crossroad, 1989)

GB   Hans-Dieter Mutschler, ed., *Gott neu buchstabieren* (Würzburg: Echter, 1994)

GM   Bernd Jochen Hilberath, *Karl Rahner. Gottgeheimnis Mensch* (Mainz: Matthias-Grünewald, 1995)

GP   Elmar Klinger, ed., *Glaube im Prozess. Christsein nach dem II. Vatikanum. Für Karl Rahner* (Freiburg: Herder, 1984)

HPT   Karl Rahner, ed., *Handbuch der Pastoraltheologie* (Freiburg: Herder, 1964–1972)

IR   Karl Rahner, *This I Remember* (New York: Crossroad, 1983)

JC   "Jesus Christ," *Theological Dictionary* (New York: Herder and Herder, 1965) 236–42 (revised translation)

KRB   *Karl Rahner, Bilder eines Lebens* (Freiburg: Herder, 1985)

KRD   Paul Imhof and Harvey Egan, *Karl Rahner in Dialogue. Conversations and Interviews, 1965–1982* (New York: Crossroad, 1986)

KRG   Paul Imhof, Hubert Biallowons, eds., *Karl Rahner im Gespräch*, 2 vols. (Munich: Kösel, 1982)

MS   *Mysterium Salutis*, 5 vols. (Einsiedeln: Benziger, 1965–1978)

R   "Revelation," *Theological Dictionary* (New York: Herder and Herder, 1965) 409–13 (revised translation)

SGG Herbert Vorgrimler, ed., *Karl Rahner. Sehnsucht nach dem geheimnisvollen Gott. Profil—Bilder—Texte* (Freiburg: Herder, 1990)

SGW Nikolaus Schwerdtfeger, *Gnade und Welt* (Freiburg: Herder, 1982)

TEG Mario Delgado, Matthias Lutz-Bachmann, eds. *Theologie aus Erfahrung der Gnade. Annäherungen an Karl Rahner* (Berlin: Morus, 1994)

TI Karl Rahner, *Theological Investigations,* 1–23

TS *Theological Studies*

VGG Karl Lehmann, ed., *Vor dem Geheimnis Gottes den Menschen verstehen. Karl Rahner zum 80. Geburtstag* (Munich: Schnell & Steiner, 1984)

VKR Herbert Vorgrimler, *Understanding Karl Rahner: An Introduction to His Life and Thought* (New York: Crossroad, 1986)

WT Herbert Vorgrimler, ed., *Wagnis Theologie* (Freiburg: Herder, 1979)

Chapter 1

A Guide to Karl Rahner's Theology

In a time of change, in a time of renewal, Karl Rahner's theology has taught believers around the world. Stimulated by what was occurring in church and culture, he employed and tamed modernity, rejected restorations of the recent past, and liberated the present for the future. Particularly in the years after 1960, his theology touched churches and schools, social activists and mystics, and countless theologians. Johann Baptist Metz wrote: "Karl Rahner renewed the face of our theology. Nothing is now as it was before him. . . . Even those who criticize him are fueled by his insights, insightful and moving perceptions about the world of life and faith."[1] Through an outpouring of theological investigations, he led others to think creatively and traditionally about God, Christ, the human person, and the church. Recently a German theologian looking at him from the perspective of new generations wrote:

> Rahner was a figure of destiny for theology in the twentieth century in Germany and beyond. He took up anew the modern world which many wished to ignore. Divine providence gave him various gifts for accomplishing great things. He was the most gifted speculative mind of the past century . . . , and yet he was unambitious to the point of forgetting about himself even as he pursued an inexhaustible production of writings and lectures. . . . He launched a landslide in theology because he was at the right place at the right time.[2]

An American observer of recent decades of intellectual life in the church concluded that the Jesuit was "one of the most outstanding and venturesome theologians of our times."[3] In 2004, a flood of books and articles celebrated the one hundredth anniversary of his birth.[4]

I. AN IMPORTANT THEOLOGIAN

Karl Rahner has been the most important Catholic theologian of the years since the 1960s. Yves Congar was an extraordinarily important thinker before the ecumenical council, Vatican II, for the council to some extent pursued Congar's own agenda of the church's renewal and Christian unity.[5] Rahner became well known in German-speaking Catholicism in the 1950s, and a wider influence began with the years during and after the council. The lives of the Dominican and the Jesuit in terms of thinking and publishing were different (both theologians went rapidly from the condition of being condemned by Vatican officials to being nominated by popes as advisers at the ecumenical council). As a young man, Congar had published pioneering works on ecumenism and ecclesiology, while Rahner's productivity surfaced more slowly; Congar's writings after the council were largely drawn from his past work, while Rahner, after he was seventy, still brought his creativity to dozens of topics in Christianity. The years after the council gave Rahner not only a wider audience but stimulated more and more books and articles in an effort lasting up to his death.

Karl Rahner showed theologians how to be Catholic and modern and helped Christians see their faith and church in a deeper and broader way. "Theology has always been devoted to giving access to the realities of faith for people who live out their lives in their own understanding of self and world in a particular age."[6] Writings prepared for and after Vatican II, the extensive translations of his work, and his impact on foreign students who studied with him and became influential in their own countries explain the lasting influence, an influence confirmed by the honorary volumes composed for his anniversary years. In 1960 Johann Auer wrote of his "ability to draw concrete realities and truths into the sphere of an idea, to let a fruitful point of departure and source pass through a long network of thoughts and consequences into practical dimensions of life."[7] In 1970 Herbert Vorgrimler began a volume of essays on the "risk of doing theology" by mentioning his "enormous productivity and the varied impulses given by that effort to theology and reaching far beyond theology."[8] In 1980 the introduction to a commemorative volume of essays treating the Jesuit theologian at Vatican II began: "Karl Rahner was not only a peritus of the Council. He belongs to those who prepared for it. He found the Council to be ultimately the representative of his great concerns, to be an advocate of a theology of humanity."[9] Recently, in 2004, Karl Neufeld gathered essays to show how Rahner's theology continues to "lead people to a responsible and relevant reflection upon Gospel and faith, a theology within the great public life of the people of God."[10]

Colloquia at Innsbruck, Austria, survey his influence through essays and bibliographies, while in North America a Karl Rahner society indicates that younger theologians who had no personal contact with Rahner are numerous.[11] Rahner's writings have been translated into many languages, Portugese and Danish, Japanese, and Indonesian. Herbert Vorgrimler observes that in Europe and North America "central statements of Rahner's have become so established among interested Christians that many people do not realize how much they owe to Rahner."[12] He gives the examples of grace as trinitarian presence, the universal will of God for salvation, and the sacraments understood as realizations of Christian existence. Despite the disdain of Vatican bureaucrats, a few bishops, and an occasional reactionary essayist, the influence of Rahner remains extensive.

II. A LASTING INFLUENCE

Karl Rahner was an unassuming figure who never sought importance or fame. He held the interest of academics and intellectuals but spoke to all kinds of people in society and church. "His theology," Neufeld concluded,

> entered in a particular way into people's lives. . . . In his own way he let the ordinariness of human life meet the Christian mystery so that every aspect of life could be penetrated by that mystery. Above all he recalled forcefully the clarity of what is Christian, of what contribution Christian faith could make to an age that often did not get beyond problematics and frameworks of questions.[13]

His importance perdures as decades pass, partly because an age distinguished by important theologians, artists, or scientists is not followed immediately by equally imposing figures, and partly because the pontificate of John Paul II encouraged an intellectually superficial Catholicism of past devotions. Neufeld sees Rahner as a contemporary theologian, indeed, a "Genosse der Zeit," "a contemporary of time itself,"[14] while Vorgrimler points out how Rahner, situating the person and her world within the presence and love of God, pursued enthusiastically new issues taking temporality and human life seriously.[15]

The influence of Karl Rahner in the United States is significant. Americans who studied with him in Germany and their students, along with countless readers of his books, have brought his thought to Catholic universities, colleges, and theology schools. Americans have

produced many articles and books on him, ranging from a comparison
with Wittgenstein to a dialogue with Hispanic Catholicism. A North
American Karl Rahner Society meets yearly and publishes the papers
delivered.[16] Volumes of his essays are becoming available in a CD-ROM
format, while websites offer bibliographical assistance. Why has a philosophical German influenced the United States? To begin, his philosophy
of existence and subject responds to the psychological world of America where philosophy is largely psychology; his acceptance of change
in church forms explains the renewal of parish life, and his perspective
of retaining what is basic in church forms while accepting realities of
participation and diversity aids the thinking of American ecclesiolo-
gists, canonists, and pastoral theologians. Why this lasting influence?
Because he honestly and creatively reconsidered many aspects of the
Christian faith and church life from the point of view of the individual
man or woman living amid the unseen worlds of grace and doubt.

III. RAHNER AND MUNICH IN THE 1960s: A PERSONAL ENCOUNTER

In 1963, just ordained a priest at the Dominican theology school
in Iowa, I came across the first volume of Karl Rahner's collected essays, *Theological Investigations* (in German *Schriften zur Theologie*), in
a translation by a British Dominican; during my seven years of seminary studies in philosophy and theology I had not heard of him. Then
suddenly I was sent to Munich for doctoral studies and learned from
Time that Rahner would be joining the faculty at the university there. In
Munich I purchased Rahner's two early works. *Spirit in the World,* his
dissertation analyzing a few pages from Aquinas's *Summa Theologiae*
on knowing in light of Kantian philosophy, didn't interest me, for I was
tired of neo-Scholastic concepts. The second book, *Hearer of the Word,*
was something new, an inquiry into the conditions for a revelation from
God to us: human knowing, freedom, language, and historicity compose
a grammar through which the Word of God can and does speak silently
even as it stimulates the emergence of human words and convictions
about who God is. "The human being is that being who in the free love
of God stands before the God of a possible revelation . . . , the being
who opens itself in free love to this revelatory message of a speaking or
silent God."[17] Revelation comes to persons who are free to respond to it;
arriving in their history, it becomes word and action and person in interplay with others. Revelation in the Bible is neither a celestial language
nor a religious myth but an increasingly explicit narrative—its climax is

Jesus of Nazareth—of what at all times is a special, silent, constant presence. Christianity should and can take into consideration the individual, the surrounding culture, and history.

As he turned sixty, Rahner arrived to join the faculty of the University of Munich in May 1964 to be Romano Guardini's successor in an interdisciplinary professorship of "Philosophy of Religion and Christian World-View." This marked the ascent of a worldwide influence and an increase in productivity.[18] To hear his opening lecture, I entered the university's main building and found a seat in the crowded *Auditorium Maximum*. A short figure in black suit and tie began to describe his intention to unfold the most basic ideas of Catholic Christianity. This course (open to all the university) offered a first version of his theological system, a theology taking the modern world seriously. Rahner appeared during his lecture as both meditative and energetic; he was, I would learn, unassuming but also passionate, speaking to students of theology—and the church and the world. His resonant voice expressed a respect for the subject of his course which he inevitably stated to be "that infinite, ineffable Mystery which in both silence and power is always secretly contacting each and every human being." Somehow I kept a few pages of my notes from that opening lecture in Munich in the spring of 1964. "The student," I wrote down during his opening lecture, "has a responsibility to understand courageously the intellectual and cultural powers of the time." Those lectures appeared in 1976 as *Foundations of Christian Faith*. The course and book bore the subtitle, "An Introduction to the Idea of Christianity," and the "idea" of Christianity recalled great thinkers of the nineteenth century like F.W.J. Schelling, J. S. Drey, and F. A. Staudenmaier. The course reflected on the totality of Christianity as something unfolding from a single seminal theme, what Jesus called the kingdom of God.[19] To hear Rahner was to hear someone who believed deeply, someone who could think and who liked to think. You felt his words and ideas were pointing to something deeper; not to a theory but to a reality, to the self but also to the active presence of God.

On other days, down the hall from the large auditorium, Rahner held weekly seminars. These were not a dozen doctoral students discussing an overly researched paper, for in the winter semester 1965/66, well over a hundred and fifty people were seated in the large slanted classroom to learn about "The Theology of Non-Belief." Perhaps because of his obligations at the council or because he wanted to repeat his practice at Innsbruck of wide-ranging discussions, those hours were an opportunity to hear Rahner think out loud on a range of topics. Which themes should we consider? One seminal and significant topic followed another. The thoughtful but engaging German voice pondered aloud what "sacrament" or "creed" or "penance for sins" might mean. For instance, peace has many dimensions and changing forms, while the meaning of "battle" and "war" is not so simple.

> Theologians in terms of peace and war should be careful, for there have been times when Christians more or less for a peace of the grave advocated war, and other times when they developed a pseudo-Christian ideology to maintain at all cost the peace of the citizenry. There are modern anti-Christian ideologies where the only realistic form of peace is the same as terror. All this shows how changeable the form and reality of peace can be.[20]

Theology, the mind and voice implied, is historical discovery and cultural insight.

Rahner, modest and approachable, did not fit the type of the *"Herr Professor."* He had no interest in prestige or in power; in interviews he described his life as without anything distinctive, the life not of an academic or an ecclesiastic but of an ordinary person working to make the Gospel credible to the people he met. What I did not know was that Rahner was forthright and irrepressible, interested in people and intrigued with new areas for free theological discussion.

> He wanted to help people, even if principles and regulations were violated as a result. He hated pious affectation, but self-righteous certainty even more. He was a freedom-loving man and could discover areas of freedom even where the official line had long regarded everything as regulated or prohibited. . . . Bishops approached Rahner's superiors in the Order to make known their discontent and obtained partial prohibitions against him. Church organizers were given hints to stop inviting Rahner.[21]

In 1965 the English-speaking doctoral students in Munich founded an association for their ever increasing number. We would invite a professor to an officers' club at a United States Army base where he would give a brief talk followed by questions. In that way the faculty would come to see that American students were serious. One time Rahner came. Toward the end of the evening his *Assistent,* Karl Lehmann, turned to me and asked if he had understood correctly that there was to be a small honorarium. I replied that there was a hundred German marks (then about twenty-five dollars). He asked if it were possible to have it that night. "You see, we are driving to Innsbruck tomorrow and we're leaving early and we don't have enough money for gas." When I showed my surprise, he replied that they never had any money because all of Rahner's salary, fees, and royalties went directly to the Society of Jesus, and the professor never remembered to ask for money. I had the impression that the overworked and little-paid Lehmann was often providing money for gas and ice cream.

It was only after teaching for a few years in the midst of the post-conciliar renewal that I slowly came to notice what I had gained and retained, some of it unconsciously, from Rahner.[22] Two aspects stood out: how to interpret the forms of a church in change, and how to glimpse grace in a wider world. The Rahnerian theology of grace illumined my world in the United States in the 1960s as the ideologies and structures of many institutions (Catholic Church, religious life and diocese, American religion with a WASP hegemony, university, military, government, business) were being critiqued and changed. Boundaries were shifting. How to explain the similarity and synchronicity of these upheavals? What did religion serve? How was it that people sometimes became selfless precisely by leaving organized religion, while some church leaders were willing to sacrifice Christian prophets and servants to preserve the status quo? The religious identities of people in the world were complex; Catholic, Methodist, and agnostic religious stances were different, but their commitment to aspects of human and political life might be the same.

I did not, however, notice that Rahner's thinking was influencing me, although he did help me see, even in 1965, that the challenges facing Catholicism were more than absorbing some insights from the Protestant Reformers or modern philosophers. Catholicism faced ecclesial renewal, late modernity, and globalization, as the social upheavals of the 1960s, critical of the Enlightenment and of existentialism, had brought a new romanticism and communitarianism. Neufeld observed: "Rahner was independent, self-assured and for that reason always interesting. As the years passed he more strongly took up his own ideas and approaches, and his development had an unmistakably personal quality."[23]

IV. A GUIDE TO A THEOLOGIAN FOR TODAY AND TOMORROW

This book aspires to be a guide to the theology of Karl Rahner. (There have been many fine introductions and studies in German and a few in English.) Avoiding academic intricacies while offering some resources in English and a few publications in German, it hopes to attract beginners and disciples, to present his theology as something fresh and helpful, and to treat important but less-noticed themes like Scripture and ministry. Do his insights and theological principles still contribute to Catholic life today? Does his thinking about the event of Jesus Christ escape the language and context of a particular time a few decades past? Topics like modernity, ministry, grace, and the world religions argue that Rahner's theology remains important. The goal of the following brief chapters is to express what is basic and original, and to inquire into how that expression of faith speaks to the beginning of a new century.[24]

To introduce, *intra-ducere*—these pages would guide readers into and within a way of thinking about Christianity. A person meeting a theologian needs to know something of his time and culture, of his teachers, and of the people he sought to address. Theology—most great theologians described and did theology in this way—lives between God's revelation and human culture, between faith and life. As theologians from Paul Tillich to Edward Schillebeeckx point out, theology is neither dogma nor sociology but a correlation of God's revelation to men and women, accepting and describing a power and a presence in people not detected by scientific instruments. Theology expresses the Word of God in human words, makes the Good News attractive in new times. Theology is not novel terms or shocking conclusions, not secular psychology or academic theory, and Rahner's lectures and publications hold no radical statements about Jesus or the papacy, for they are inevitably about something beneath the things and texts of Christianity: the real presence of God in history. To some extent everyone is a theologian, and in his last years Rahner observed that for him writing and speaking ended not in footnoted articles but in the expression for ordinary people of what was most basic in the Gospel.

How should one read a great theologian? The wrong introduction renders a theologian dry and tedious, turns intellectual challenge into boredom. To encounter a theologian is to enter into his vision, to feel something of her energy. We do meet a thinker in past writings, although we should not hand our intellectual pursuit over to a diffident reading of printed texts. We read the pages holding the perspectives of a metaphysician or a mystic to find in them a luminous access to the real. Texts are only guides and witnesses to life. To understand a theology of some import begins with grasping its underlying themes.

A dull or misguided teacher can transform Rahner and the exciting history of Catholicism in the twentieth century into something distant or irrelevant, while a reactionary or fundamentalist mentality will turn thinking itself into something unorthodox or dangerous. There are ways not to study great thinkers. It is preferable not to study them solely on one's own, for then shallow or incorrect interpretations may replace teaching. An initial understanding of a thinker takes some time, and a mature interpretation requires years. A great artist or physicist is more than a source of information to be stored. I once asked a class why important modern theologians and philosophers were difficult to understand. The answer came back: "Because they wrote in German!" Rahner's German is supposed to be difficult—certainly the sentences are long.[25] His process of thinking, however, is straightforward; the often brief and logical sentences are direct. A theologian does not have an endless string of new ideas but a few insights—insights appearing with their own language and perspective, a few new insights and terms and themes. The writings of an Aristotle or a Kant offer not so much facts as perspectives, ways of understanding self and society. Great minds are difficult because they offer a new viewpoint through a kind of code: the code is found in the thought-forms expressing ideas drawn from a culture and a time. The code offers not esoteric metaphors from the libraries of academia but insights into the real world. What makes a thinker, a theologian perduring? Their words and ideas make sense of my experience of my world, make sense of the world in its own proper historical forms at this time. A thinker is great because writings offer a new perspective about the human and the divine. How should I live on this planet and at this time in history? Where lies my destiny? Is there an unseen God, and how does a supreme being relate to me? Theologians employ philosophies, aesthetics, psychologies, or sociologies not to prove the content of Jesus' revelation but to express the Word and its words to a particular culture in a striking way. Jesus' revelation is not so much about a divine being as about God personally engaged with us, and a theologian is a theoretician of life and history within the mystery of a special divine presence. "Christology, theology and anthropology are so intimately connected that it would help bring out the true idea of anthropocentric theology by calling it 'incarnational.'"[26]

Curiously, the time spent in learning about one person's world somehow aids the appreciation of others. To study one great artist or thinker is to see and understand a little about other great scientists, thinkers, and artists. Rahner is never sectarian, never closed, never antiquarian; he is not interested in propping up a clerical caste or an academic society. His theology of the horizon of grace reaching out through history, prior to statues and rituals, is the opposite of any fundamentalism. His understanding of history shows how trying to restore the recent past is doomed: no one lives there, and the forms restored obscure the potential within great theologies and liturgies of the past.[27] The Jesuit often repeated that a theologian is really being a theologian not when he assigns dogmatic propositions places in a syllogism but when he reexperiences the depth in Jesus teaching, when he sees how history draws forth from word and sacrament both a yes and a no because both rest over the abyss of the inexpressibility of God. As people learn about Rahner's ideas, they often mention that they themselves had thought something similar for years.

How should one approach this theology? How should one read Karl Rahner? His theology is well known for managing to be both personal and global. Christians find there variety and simplicity, a myriad of topics in a context of personal life, a history of humanity surrounded by grace leading to Jesus Christ, and an openness to diversity, ministry, sacrament, and participation in the church.[28]

* * *

What lasts and remains great is fully immersed in its own age and yet transcends it. This theology will live on when much contemporary theological literature is forgotten.[29] Rahner himself is a good guide to his writings, and his writings illumine each other. His pleasure and openness in giving interviews, his tendency to explain his viewpoints in light of past and present movements in society and church, suggest approaching him through his personal comments. "Theology," he wrote,

> is a reflection upon revealed Christian faith. This reflection stands in the service of the Church so that it can fulfill its job of preaching, as well as it can, so that it reaches the contemporary person. . . . Theology has the job of a dialogue with the contemporary person's understanding of self and world; beyond that it has the job of being a worldwide theology, developing a Latin America, East Asian, and African theology.[30]

A representative of a newer generation of independent theologians learning from Rahner, Bernd Jochen Hilberath, sums up:

> We can trace the significance of Karl Rahner for contemporary theology in two ways. First, research can look at the development, the conditions, the main themes and the unresolved difficult issues, drawing on basic principles and future-oriented ideas. . . . The second way begins in the world of today and asks what are the frameworks and motifs in theology being pursued today. What are the main themes and difficulties of today's theology? Then a dialogue between the historical situation and the theology of Rahner is developed.[31]

This introduction, written two decades after Karl Rahner's death, is inevitably a reexpression and at times an application drawing a past theology to the present and the future. This retelling of an influential theology cannot avoid including somewhat my interpretation, and I ask for indulgence if my words become prominent.

* * *

Someone is riding from an airport into the heart of a large city, a city like Los Angeles or New York, Lagos or Tokyo—in many classes I have pointed out the lasting importance of Karl Rahner's theology with this image and experience.

You look out through the window and see countless people busy about their lives. Are they religious? Are they Christians? Many are, many are not, depending on global geography. Many may be members of other religions, while others have left any formal religious group. And yet, are they not all seeking life, seeking meaning and transcendence? They accept and fashion the direction of their daily life by some kind of faith, love, and hope regardless of what they name these. What do I make of them? Does their church, synagogue, mosque exhaust the religious dimensions of their life? Or does their relationship to grace and sin, to God's love and God's plan for the race of planet earth lie deeper? A few Christians may follow, because it is clear and simple, a negative fundamentalism, and send billions of men and women who are not members of this or that particular church to a hell. That would be a startling decision for a God of love. Is it not more likely from Jesus' teaching that no people are left out of the force of divine? No creatures are frustrated or damned prior to their lives, and yet, there is no neutral park for people where they would exist outside of a saving history of God's presence. An alternative theology shows how all that Jesus called the kingdom of God contacts and influences people living before and outside of the Gospel even while Jesus Christ remains the light of the world.

* * *

This theology the following chapters sketch.

NOTES

1. Metz, *Den Glauben lehren und denken. Dank an Karl Rahner* (Munich: Kösel, 1984) 13.

2. Dieter Hattrup, "Karl Rahner zum Hundertsten," *Theologie und Glaube* 94 (2004) 551; see the insightful introduction of Michael Schulz, *Karl Rahner begegnen* (Augsburg: Sankt Ulrich, 2004).

3. Charles Meyer, "Karl Rahner: A Theologian for Our Time," *Chicago Studies* 43 (2004) 239; for personal reflections see William F. Bell, "Rambling with Rahner," *America* 173 (1994) 14, 15, 18; Gregory Raftery, "Rahner in the Gaeltacht," *Spirituality* 11:1 and 2 (2005) 54–9, 139–41; Barbara Finan, "Rahner's Place," *Ohio Dominican College Scene* (Winter 2001) 24–5. Melvin Michalski and Andreas Batlogg have just published a collection of several dozen interviews with Rahner's friends and students: *Begegnungen mit Karl Rahner. Weggefährten erinnern sich* (Freiburg: Herder, 2006).

4. For instance, *The Courage to Risk Everything. Essays Marking the Centenary of Karl Rahner's Birth.* Louvain Studies 29 (2004); *Karl Rahner 100 Jahre Zeitschrift für Katholische Theologie* 126 (2004); and special issues of *Stimmen der Zeit* for 2004 and of *Gregorianum* (2005).

5. On his early sense of a vocation to renew the church through historical and ecumenical work see "Letter from Yves Congar, o.p.," *Theology Digest* 32:3 (1985) 213. At the end of Vatican II, he wrote in his diary: "I left the Basilica slowly and with difficulty; a number of bishops congratulated me, saying that this was very much my work. Looking at things objectively, I did do a lot to prepare for the Council, to elaborate and diffuse the ideas the Council made its own. At the Council itself I worked a lot." He lists the sections of Constitutions on the Church and Revelation that are from him, the introduction and the conclusion of the documents on Ecumenism, non-Christian, foreign missions, priests, and religious liberty. "In short, this morning, that which was read came very extensively from me" (Congar, *Mon Journal du Concile* II [Paris: Cerf, 2002] 510f.).

6. "Grundsätzliche Überlegungen zur Anthropologie und Protologie im Rahmen der Theologie," *MS* 2 406.

7. Johann Auer, "Das Werk Karl Rahners," *Theologische Revue* 60 (1964) 147.

8. "Ein Brief zur Einführung," *WT* 11.

9. Elmar Klinger, "Vorwort," *GP* 5.

10. Neufeld, "Erinnerung," *Karl Rahner 100 Jahre. Zeitschrift für katholische Theologie* 126 (2004) 1f.

11. Roman Siebenrock, ed., *Karl Rahner in der Diskussion* (Innsbruck: Tyrolia, 2001) summarizes the influence of Rahner's theology around the world. From meetings held in 1993 and 1999 in Innsbruck, the volume holds over twenty essays on topics such as church office, Maurice Blondel, ecclesiology, neo-Scholasticism, etc., by figures like Reisenhofer, Möbs, Rulands, Tourenne, and others; see, on the contemporary dialogue with Rahner, Andreas Batlogg, "Karl Rahner im Gespräch," *Zeitschrift für katholische Theologie* 121 (1999) 431ff. In 1989 a decision was made to issue a new edition of much of Rahner's writings. This would publish better editions of some writings and first editions of unpublished works. Since then a number of volumes have appeared (not in their numerical order), volumes on pastoral theology, on creation, on the church fathers (see Albert Raffelt, "Was will die Karl Rahner-Gesamtausgabe?" *Zeitschrift für Katholische Theologie* 121 [1999] 413–30).

12. *VKR* 110; see Declan Marmion and Mary Hines, *The Cambridge Companion to Karl Rahner* (Cambridge: Cambridge University Press, 2005). For Rahner's influence in Francophone theology, see Jean-Claude Petit, "La Réception de la pensée et de l'oeuvre de Karl Rahner dans la théologie française," *Science et Esprit* 53 (2001) 353–73. On Rahner's influence in Croatia see Živan Bezić, "Nezaboravljeni Rahner," *Ephemerides theologicae Zagrabnenses* 74 (2004) 289–96; in the Czech Republic, Michael Altrichter, "Die Rahner-Rezeption in Boehmen," *Stimmen der Zeit* 131 (2006) 196–201; in Russia, P. Modesto, "Transzendentalanthropologie und Materialismus. Aufnahme und Kritik Karl Rahners in der Sowjetunion," *WT* 132ff. A collection of essays in Spanish appeared for his seventieth birthday, A. Vargas-Machuca, ed., *Teologia y Mundo Contemporaneo* (Madrid: Ediciones Cristiandad, 1974), and for the anniversary of his death, *Estudios Eclesiásticos* 80 (2005). For

Asia there is Tamás Nyíri, *Theologie in Ost und West*. *Karl Rahners Beitrag* (Frankfurt: Lang, 1996) and pages on Rahner's presence in India and Japan in *KRB*, 153–7, while on Africa see René de Haes, "Einfluss auf die Jungen Ortskirche in Afrika," in Paul Imhof and Hubert Biallowons, eds., *KRB*, 150–3.

13. Neufeld "Karl Rahner—Zeitgenosse," *GB* 35.

14. Ibid., 14.

15. Herbert Vorgrimler, "Zur bleibenden Aktualität Karl Rahners," *Theologische Revue* 100 (2004) 91–100; see *Gotteserfahrung in Leben und Denken* (Darmstadt: Primus, 2004). For a survey of Rahner literature in the last decade see Bernhard Nitsche, "Bilanz-Umbrüche-Desiderate. Rahner-Forschungsbericht 1995–2004, 2 Teile," *Theologische Quartalschrift* 185 (2005) 303–19; 186 (2006) 4–15.

16. Wide-ranging articles on Rahner appear in the special yearly issue of *Philosophy & Theology;* see Michael Fahey's address to the Catholic Theological Society that documents his influence in the United States ("Presidential Address: 1904–1984, Karl Rahner, Theologian," *Proceedings, Catholic Theological Society* 39 [1984] 84–98); John Padberg, "Einfluss auf die Theologie in den Vereinigten Staaten," *Karl Rahner. Bilder eines Lebens,* 114–7. Recent studies with original perspectives include Miguel Diaz, *On Being Human. U.S. Hispanic and Rahnerian Perspectives* (Maryknoll, NY: Orbis, 2001); Terrence W. Klein, *How Things Are in the World. Metaphysics and Theology in Wittgenstein and Rahner* (Milwaukee: Marquette University Press, 2004); Michael Purcell, *Mystery and Method. The Other in Rahner and Levinas* (Milwaukee: Marquette University Press, 1998); Michael Petty, *A Faith that Loves the Earth: The Ecological Theology of Karl Rahner* (Lanham, MD: University Press of America, 1996); John J. O'Donnell, *Life in the Spirit* (Rome: Editrice Gregoriana, 2004). Recently there have appeared too the papers of the conference, "Rahner at the Pacific Rim" (Franklin, WI: Sheed & Ward, 2005).

17. *Hörer des Wortes* (Freiburg: Herder, 1963) 133, 9; see T. O'Meara, *A Theologian's Journey* (New York: Paulist Press, 2002) chs. 6 and 7.

18. Bernhard Welte, "Ein Vorschlag zur Methode der Theologie heute," *Gott in Welt* 1 (Freiburg: Herder, 1964) 285.

19. *F* 1, 4. Mark Fischer has published a helpful abridged version, an accessible English paraphrase of *Foundations of Christian Faith* with introduction and indices, *The Foundations of Karl Rahner* (New York: Crossroad, 2005).

20. "The Peace of God and the Peace of the World," *TI* 10, 372.

21. *UKR* 87.

22. In 1970 I published a theology of that volatile time, *Loose in the World,* some of which was a popularization of Rahner. Later a reviewer noticed how the underlying structure of some of the chapters of *Theology of Ministry* was indebted to him. On Rahner and teaching theology, see the essays in *Philosophy & Theology* 11 (1998) 191–205; Georg Baudler, "Göttliche Gnade und Menschliches Leben. Religionspädagogische Aspekte der Offenbarungs- und Gnadentheologie Karl Rahners," *WT* 35–50l; Roman Bleistein, "Mystagogie und Religionspädagogik," *WT* 51–60.

23. Karl Neufeld, "Karl Rahner—Zeitgenosse," *GB* 20.

24. Robert Kress offers helpful suggestions in "How to Read Rahner," *A Rahner Handbook* (Atlanta: John Knox Press, 1982) 93–7; see George Vass, *Understanding*

Karl Rahner in Two Volumes: The Mystery of Man and the Foundations of a Theological System and *A Theologian in Search of a Philosophy* (Westminster, PA: Christian Classics, 1985). Essays guiding the student through the *Foundations* are found in Leo O'Donovan, ed., *A World of Grace* (New York: Seabury, 1980).

25. Did Rahner have some poor pedagogical habits? There was the assembly of qualifications, the distracting repetition of a phrase or idea over a few pages, the move from one topic to a different one. That style, in Franz Mayr's view, is a proper and positive aspect of Rahner's writings: The German language tends to a mode of thinking and speaking both synthetic and cyclical. Regardless, Rahner's style of writing and speaking is very much his style of thinking (Franz K. Mayr, "Vermutungen zu Karl Rahners Sprachstil," in *WT* 143, 137); see Karl Neumann, "Sprache und Stil," *GB* 24–39; Herbert Vorgimler, "Zum Sprachstil," *S* (Darmstadt: Primus, 2004) 5–9. If this style can hinder Americans, the impression should not be given that abstract phrases are theology. Lehmann notes the interplay in his thought between a questioning and a seeking spirit. The many essays with their long introductions look at topics and their histories from different directions. In the relationships of the divine and human, the historical and the personal, the philosophical and the pastoral, categories and systems are tested to see if they can illumine contemporary questions. Inevitably a liberating idea appears, an insight to be followed to its consequences ("Karl Rahner zum Gedächtnis," *Stimmen der Zeit* 212 [1994] 147–50).

26. *KRD* 19.

27. Rahner mentions two dead ends; a narrow fundamentalism and an esoteric theatricality; both fixate on language or ritual in a superficial way of conceiving the church's mission in the world ("Church and the World," *SM* 1, 348–51).

28. See the pastoral topics treated in Karl Neumann, *Der Praxisbezug der Theologie bei Karl Rahner* (Freiburg: Herder, 1980) 7–12.

29. As Joseph Ratzinger observed in a review of *Foundations* when it first appeared (*Theologische Revue* 74 [1978] 177ff.).

30. *KRD* 324.

31. *GM* 13; on new generations of theologians drawing on Rahner, see Andreas Batlogg, "Generationenwechsel oder: Wem gehört Karl Rahner?" *Zeitschrift für Katholische Theologie* 115 (1993) 451–3.

Chapter 2

Karl Rahner, Theologian

Karl Rahner was a German Catholic, a Jesuit, a teacher, a writer. He was a preacher and thinker of human life, divine presence, and sacramental community. Karl Neufeld, professor at the University of Innsbruck, says simply that he was "one of the greatest German Catholic Theologians of the past hundred years,"[1] while Karl Lehmann—Rahner's *Assistent* in Munich in the 1960s, then professor at Mainz, and subsequently the leader of the German bishops' conference and cardinal—concluded: "Karl Rahner belongs to the great pioneers of the renewal of Catholic theology in our century."[2] At the time of Rahner's death, John Galvin wrote of "a Rahner revolution,"[3] a revolution enabling Catholics to think in the culture of late modernity but also a revolution disclosing long ignored insights of Paul or Thomas Aquinas or Ignatius Loyola. Herbert Vorgrimler wrote: "The depth and goal of all of this theological production are its variety and comprehensiveness; the diversity in the theological life-work of Karl Rahner corresponds to the variety of themes in the Christian faith."[4] Varied themes, developed in a brief meditation or a long article, drew forth an imaginative treatment, an approach asking what past words and present forms of some Christian reality meant, and what it might mean today. Rahner looked at the totality of Christianity and at its individual aspects. He mediated between old and new theologies even as he developed an original perspective. He treated concrete issues by looking at their biblical sources, historical development, and contemporary meaning. After age sixty he remained creative.

> Open to an astonishing degree . . . , there was a certain discontent or restlessness. . . . He always took a question in different directions. . . . His popularity came about because he responded to post-conciliar change in the Catholic Church. The most speculative was the most practical."[5]

15

I. AN ORDINARY LIFE

Karl Rahner, born in Freiburg im Breisgau on March 5, 1904, was one of seven children.[6] That area around Freiburg reaches up through the Black Forest to the source of the Danube. The home of the Allemanen tribe mentioned by Julius Caesar, it has been well known for its production of speculative minds; to the east is the Swabia of Schiller, Hegel, and Schelling; to the west the cantons of Albert Schweitzer, Karl Barth, and Hans Küng. Rahner's father was an assistant principal in a teacher's college. His mother—her family were innkeepers—lived to the age of 101 (she advised her son when he retired in his seventies not to work so hard and to leave theological controversy to the younger generation). Rahner belonged to the youth movement directed by Romano Guardini. "It was more a grass-roots than a church-directed affair. But it was Catholic, religious, extremely active and intense. There I was influenced positively in many ways that affected my future life, especially since that was when I first met Romano Guardini at Castle Rothenfels."[7] After his completion of the Gymnasium course in 1922, Rahner entered the novitiate of one of the German provinces of the Society of Jesus in Feldkirch (Voralberg), Austria (his brother Hugo had entered three years earlier). After taking vows in 1924, Rahner spent his first year of philosophy at Feldkirch and two subsequent years of philosophical studies at Pullach near Munich. Here and during his years of study in theology at Valkenburg in The Netherlands he was introduced to Catholic neo-Scholastic philosophy but also to something exceptional for the Catholic Church at that time: modern philosophies. Jesuits like the Belgian Joseph Maréchal (1878–1944) and the French Jesuit Pierre Rousselot (1878–1915) had begun a dialogue between Thomas Aquinas and Immanuel Kant. Aristotle and Aquinas, like Kant, had appreciated the activity of the personality, the mind's intuition moving beyond things to some Infinite. Rahner also observed the career of Erich Przywara, a Jesuit of synthesis who anticipated Rahner's efforts in some ways. Przywara's sources were Aquinas and Newman, Scheler and Ignatius Loyola, whom he employed to further a dialogue between German Catholicism after 1919 and Protestantism and modern thought and art. Rahner said of Przywara: "What is proper, almost unique in his work is that he is Catholic in a real, life-long dialogue with the past and the present, with the entire European intellectual history from Heraclitus to Nietzsche. He opens himself to all and can give to all."[8]

Jesuit formation included a time of ministerial internship, and from 1927 to 1929 Rahner taught Latin to the novices at Feldkirch, an exercise leading to a certain mastery of Latin that would be helpful in dealing with the history of theology and later with composing drafts of documents at Vatican II. One of the novices in the Latin class was Alfred Delp, who later was in the Kreisauer circle working against Hitler. Arrested by the Nazis on July 28, 1944, he pronounced his final Jesuit vows in prison and was hanged in Berlin on February 2, 1945. Rahner would later recall his friendship with Delp, whom he considered to be in "the front ranks of those witnesses who were motivated by Christianity to resist the evils of Nazism."[9] In 1929 Rahner returned to Valkenburg for theological studies, and during that time he spent a great deal of study on the fathers of the church and medieval theologians. Early publications after 1932 were on the notion of biblical interpretation in Origen and Bonaventure and on mysticism and lay ministry in patristic theologians. On July 26, 1932, he was ordained to the priesthood in the Jesuit church in Munich, St. Michael, founded by St. Peter Canisius as a center of the Counter-Reformation.

In 1934 Rahner returned to Freiburg im Breisgau to pursue a doctorate in philosophy (his superiors intended him to teach the history of philosophy at Pullach). The young Jesuit arrived in a university with a strong tradition and presence of phenomenology (Husserl, retired, lived there) and neo-Kantianism.

> I studied mainly under Martin Heidegger, already known and becoming famous. He had just been the first rector of that university under the Nazi regime, and we two young priests, J. B. Lotz and I, were not anxious to throw in our lot with him for good or for ill, and so we enrolled with the professor of Catholic scholastic philosophy, Martin Honecker. Nonetheless, our encounter with Heidegger was the decisive, impressive experience.[10]

Johannes Baptist Lotz describes the arrival of the two Jesuits at the university.

> After the conclusion of our education as Jesuits, Karl Rahner and I were to begin doctoral studies in philosophy at a German university. At that time, the beginning of the winter semester, 1934/35, only two names were of interest: Martin Heidegger and Nicolai Hartmann. We chose the first because we hoped to find in him a greater potential for thought and stimulating ideas. . . . While we attended the lectures of men like Martin Honecker, Fritz Kaufmann, Erik Wolf, and Walter Bröcker, Heidegger was the attraction that kept us in Freiburg for four semesters. Standing in front of the list of courses posted for our first semester, Rahner and I saw listed Heidegger's three hour lecture course on Hölderlin's ode

Germanien and a seminar on Hegel's *Phänomenologie des Geistes*. Next to the entry on the seminar was the qualification *"Privatissime."* Participation was possible only after a personal interview with the teacher. . . . We were admitted and were happy about that, not yet realizing what an honor it was.[11]

The Jesuits attended further courses and seminars, for instance, on Kant's second critique and Schelling's *Essay on Freedom*.

Honecker (years later I heard Rahner refer to him as *"der dumme Honecker"*) did not accept the dissertation written under his direction: the focus was too much on the active subject, and the reading of Aquinas was too creative an interpretation of precise aspects of Aquinas's epistemology seen within the transcendental Thomism of Maréchal; and the language and conceptuality were imaginative in a Heideggerian way. "I was failed by the Catholic Honecker for being too inspired by Heidegger."[12] Heidegger, however, was reluctant to involve himself in the direction of Rahner's dissertation; his neo-Kantian period was behind him. Rahner left Freiburg without a doctorate. His superiors assigned him to teach not philosophy but theology, and he wrote quickly a theological dissertation for the University of Innsbruck on an aspect of Christ's passion.[13] The rejected Freiburg dissertation became *Spirit in the World* published in 1939 and translated into other languages. Francis Fiorenza sums up:

> Whereas Kant rejected the theoretical knowledge of God for a practical postulate of God, Rahner has attempted to show the relevance of a theoretical theology for the pastoral theology and practical life of the church. This synthesis is the wisdom of Karl Rahner's theology, and its source is *Spirit in the World*.[14]

The Nazis closed the theological faculty at Innsbruck after 1938, and Rahner spent the war years involved in religious education sponsored by an early diocesan pastoral institute in Vienna and later some parish ministry in Bavaria.[15] He preached a series of sermons for Lent 1946 in the Jesuit church in bombed-out central Munich, and their published version in 1948, *On the Need and Blessing of Prayer*, sold thousands of copies. In 1948 Rahner began to teach in the reconstituted theology faculty at Innsbruck, and the essays and lectures from the 1950s were published as the first volume of *Schriften zur Theologie*[16] (*Theological Investigations*), a series of sixteen volumes (totaling around 8,000 pages) begun in 1954 and ending only with his death. Rahner edited with others a new edition of Denziger's *Enchiridion Symbolorum*, that collection of authoritative church documents from two millennia, composed a theological dictionary, and co-edited the German Catholic encyclopedia *Lexikon für Theologie und Kirche* in ten volumes with thirty thousand articles of which he wrote about 135.[17] He contributed to or edited many of the series *Quaestiones Disputatae* which at his death held over a hundred books (1958–84). Giving talks to audiences large and small, he wrote about topics as diverse as the difficulties of aging or the identity of the priest. At the same time, he was sought after as a director of retreats and as a university preacher.

Rahner was part of the renewal of church life beginning after World War II and leading to Vatican II. New attitudes toward receiving the sacraments, dialogue with non-Catholics, and issues in moral theology unfolded rapidly. Vorgrimler observes:

> To understand Karl Rahner one must also understand that he was in the second generation of theological renewal . . . [that] could no longer be content with only assertions of a new spirit but held an attitude open to the modern period with its mentality, art and problems. That new spirit would have more than a minor influence in a renewed church praxis, in new pastoral ministries and a new reformed liturgy, and so on. A new approach needed to devote itself to the whole range of individual questions in philosophy, theology, and church life, and show that the new approach was both contemporary and also of the church.[18]

Still, the 1950s were difficult years for progressive Catholic thinkers as the Vatican forbade publications with ideas that went beyond medievalism. Leading French theologians were removed from teaching and publishing in 1954. Rahner's contacts with Rome before the council had been few and negative. A study on the Assumption of Mary (proclaimed a dogma in 1950) had been forbidden publication, and at the end of 1954 Pius XII had criticized his theology on "the multiplicity of Masses and the one sacrifice," a theology that, ten years later, Rahner observed to Paul VI, had become widely accepted in the restored liturgy of concelebration.

> When the Congregation of Faith in Rome under Cardinal Ottaviani once said that I could write only in conjunction with a special Roman censor, then I said to myself: "Well, I just won't write anymore, and then the matter is over and done with, right?" But nothing came of it because the Council arrived.[19]

Over the objections of influential Jesuits at the Gregorian University, Pope John XXIII appointed him in 1961 to a commission preparing for Vatican II, although he was not invited to Rome for any of the early sessions of his group. As the opening of the council neared, bishops were permitted to select a theological adviser, and Cardinal König of Vienna chose Rahner. "Rahner," the cardinal recalled,

> was startled at first and asked to think it over; he said that he had never been in Rome, that his name was no recommendation for me, and that he feared difficulties in the place where his censures had originated. His first theological works marked by existential philosophy and new aspects of anthropology had found in many circles astonishment and criticism. After some hesitation he accepted my invitation.[20]

Rahner arrived at Vatican II as a conciliar expert in a curious situation: no time had intervened between heretical suspicion and conciliar accreditation (Konrad Adenauer was among those who signed a letter protesting the censorship of the Jesuit theologian). During the first two sessions his numerous addresses in Rome strengthened the bishops' resolve to seek out new directions.

> The schemata of the preconciliar type, put together by the Roman theologians before the Council and for the Council, were so full of neo-Scholasticism that in many ways one can really thank God they were dropped. . . . I would not say that I performed anything special that one could pin down. I did work very hard, and it was terribly tiring work. It is hard to imagine how a particular decree, in some cases after hundreds of suggestions for corrections from bishops and others, finally found a formulation that was then accepted by the Council.[21]

Rahner was drawn into an enormous amount of work, and letters back to Innsbruck and Munich spoke of slow progress through meetings and drafts; he was never seized by conciliar euphoria and later evaluated the success of the council as modest. "I got back from Rome yesterday, tired. But one can always work to see that the worst does not happen and that small points of contact for a later theology are put in the schemata. That's not much, and yet it's a great deal."[22] At the conclusion of the council, Rahner's articles and addresses as well as a commentary on all the documents sent the impact of Vatican II forward.

In the years after the council, the Jesuit's reputation expanded. In the following decade he edited and wrote large sections for the five-volume *Handbuch der Pastoraltheologie* (1964–69), the four-volume *Sacramentum Mundi* (1967–69), and a seven-volume compendium of dogmatic theology *Mysterium Salutis* (1965–76), as well as publishing a commentary on the documents of Vatican II. An array of books on theological topics, smaller works of meditations and prayers, as well as countless essays were stimulated by his involvement in the concrete life of the Catholic Church, a church in search of a diversity in the world, a church he experienced somewhat outside Austria and Germany. Many universities in Europe invited him to lecture in those years, and his writings were translated into various languages.

An inquiry came from the philosophical faculty in Munich in February 1963: Would the Jesuit entertain the idea of being Romano Guardini's successor? "I felt that this was attractive and quite an honor, because the appointment came ultimately from Romano Guardini himself."[23] Rahner arrived in Munich at the time of his sixtieth birthday, and the daily paper, the *Süddeutsche Zeitung*, published in March 1964 a long article by Heinrich Fries noting his ever-widening influence. A two-volume collection of essays *Gott in Welt* celebrated the birthday: several dozen articles in thirteen hundred pages were introduced by sixty-one pages of congratulations by theologians, bishops, and philosophers. The Jesuits Lotz and Emil Coreth wrote on modern ontology; Bernhard Welte and Otto Semmelroth treated major issues of fundamental theology like freedom and personalism. There was a posthumous contribution by Gustave Weigel that drew together Paul Tillich's method of correlation, and the address of John XXIII inaugurating Vatican II to emphasize that faith should be expressed in a language people could understand. Yves Congar examined the conciliarity of the church, while Bernard Häring considered the relationship of morality to church. Joseph Ratzinger treated the world religions and Erich Przywara wrote on Catholicism and ecumenism.

During the Munich years, work expanded yet further: new essays and books, evaluations of drafts of the conciliar documents, the direction of doctoral dissertations, the direction of a multivolume international systematic theology, all of this assisted by the tireless efforts of Karl Lehmann.[24] The professorship assumed from Guardini, however, was located in the philosophy faculty, and envious professors in theology ruled that Rahner could not direct doctoral students in theology. "I'll stay in Munich if I'm allowed to have doctoral students." As he later explained:

> For all practical purposes the theology faculty refused me this rather harmless, and in other respects, obvious and reasonable request. Then the only thing I could really say was: "Good, then I'll take the appointment to Münster." Guardini was very disappointed in me and vexed about this. Still, there was nothing I could do.[25]

In April 1967 he accepted a professorship in dogmatic theology at Münster where he taught until his retirement in 1971.

Living at Jesuit houses in Munich from 1971 to 1981 and afterwards in Innsbruck, Rahner continued lecturing and writing. In 1973 Rahner spent some time in Chile to understand liberation theology; subsequently, he went to Ireland, Switzerland, Hungary, and Spain.

In 1983 he and Heinrich Fries composed what remains a particularly creative book on ecumenism, *Unity of the Churches: An Actual Possibility.* The celebrations of his eightieth birthday in Germany and Austria, Hungary and Great Britain tired him out, but the television record of his lecture at the special convocation in Freiburg shows the lasting vitality, humility, wisdom, and humor.

> My theme is "Experiences of a Catholic Theologian." I do not mean the personal and intimate experiences which belong in a true autobiography, something I will never write. I also don't mean ecclesiastical, clerical, or ecclesiastical-political experiences, for mine seem to me not to be very important. . . . I mean the experiences of a theologian, or, better said, of a human being who was commissioned to be a theologian but who does not know so clearly if he was up to that calling.[26]

He accepted invitations from Heythrop College in London and the Budapest Academy in Hungary. All of this was preliminary to the celebration on his actual birthday on March 5th in Innsbruck.[27] Three days after the celebrations, Rahner fell ill and died a few weeks later on March 30, 1984.

II. TEACHERS AND SOURCES

Karl Rahner's theology draws on past and present theologies and is an intersection between premodern and modern forms, between European Roman Catholicism and a wider world. He studied the writings of past theologians while he experienced directly some contemporary thinkers and schools. He stood apart from each of them, altering and vivifying this or that aspect. Experts have explained how tradition and Scripture, Thomas Aquinas and contemporary life, Ignatius of Loyola and Heidegger were his sources.[28]

Rahner is a philosophical theologian, but he is not primarily a philosopher. Studies of his philosophy can obscure his theology and distract from his vocation of interpreting the Christian message. Philosophy, Aristotelian or modern German philosophy, is pursued not because it gives metaphysical axioms or logical proofs but because it is the expression of the cultural horizon of ideas, the description of how people describe themselves. Philosophy and theology express a worldview, one based on the experiences of life—the same is true of the arts, from painting to literature.[29] Like many great thinkers and artists, Karl Rahner stood at an intersection of movements and personalities.

Thomas Aquinas. Rahner was a gifted student of Aquinas: he had an extensive knowledge of Aquinas and of neo-Thomism, and he possessed a talent for expressing Aquinas in a modern conceptuality and language. Principles from Aquinas are present: the distinction between being and grace in their positive interplay; God as a generous source of supernatural life; the human person knowing and seeking the Infinite in being and grace; the gift of revelation and grace coming to human beings in their personalities.

Grace is the theme of Rahner's theological system—grace as uncreated and personal, as the Holy Spirit, and as tending to the historical and objective. Grace is also an underlying theme of the *Summa Theologiae*. It is not difficult to see a parallel between Aquinas's missions of the Trinity to earth and Rahner's self-communication of God to a human existence and its activities. The final question on the Trinity in the *Summa Theologiae* sets in motion the order of grace and salvation history on earth,[30] while the sharing of God's depths expresses that theology of Word and Spirit at work in people. Careful study of the medieval Dominican finds a limited anthropocentricity and a transcendental activity of the knowing person.[31] Even the development of a theology to deal with the billions of devotees of world religions begins with a Thomist generosity of God's gifts in creation and grace in contrast to a strict Augustinianism of corrupt natures and intrusive demons. We have learned to see that in Aquinas's christology the dynamic linking question is not one about Chalcedonian natures but the headship of Jesus: a christology of solidarity with the human family, of linking the individual who is the source of all that is grace with the lines of history, and even of the history of religions.[32] Rahner's theme of sacramentality extends the liturgical sacrament into the ministries of the church, expanding the sacramental union of sign and causality in Aquinas.

> Thomas is a mystic adoring the mystery beyond all possibility of expression. . . . Thomas knows that the highest precision and sober objective accuracy of true theology ultimately serve only one purpose: to force the individual out of the lucid clarity of his existence into the mystery of God where he no longer grasps but is grasped, where he no longer reasons but adores, where he does not master but is overpowered.[33]

Rahner exercised a relentless critique on neo-Scholasticism, the "*Schultheologie,*" dominating all seminaries and most universities throughout the Catholic world from 1860 to 1960. "School-theology" meant to Rahner two things: (1) the theology taught in seminary classrooms from 1880 to 1960 and found in seminary textbooks, manuals with blocks of information; (2) forms of neo-Scholasticism in the nineteenth and twentieth centuries. In the second, a boring, abstract system, more philosophical than Christian, addressed no important issues, spoke to no living people, and disdained human cultures. He did not consider the great figures of the Middle Ages to be well presented in that philosophical scaffolding. Precisely what was objectionable in neo-Scholasticism led to its rapid demise: the reduction of the realities of the Christian message to Latin propositions; a disdain for pastoral life; totalitarian judgment, control, and monopoly of logical exposition over the Scriptures. Neo-Scholastic textbooks in a treatment of a few pages reduced grace to actual graces, moral theology to a mechanics of sacramental action, and spirituality to methods of meditation aspiring to produce theatrical charisms. What this theological mentality saw as important were contacts between a divine pumping station and a timeless human soul.[34] Of the attitude of his generation he wrote:

> We read the works of Thomas: we allowed him to alert us to certain problems, but ultimately we approached him with our own questions and problems. And so we didn't really practice a Thomistic scholasticism but tried to maintain toward him a stance comparable to that toward Augustine, Origen, and other great thinkers.[35]

That neo-Scholasticism enveloping all of Roman Catholicism in the century before 1960, against which Rahner had to struggle, is no longer much known, although there is great interest today in Thomas Aquinas.

Modern Philosophy. Were modern philosophers only inevitable fonts of atheism and relativism? If Plato, Aristotle, and Aquinas remain thinkers from which Christians can learn, can Catholic philosophy and theology only imitate the past? Christianity cannot remain in a library or in a sacristy of statues and chalices but must look at each time in history. Idealism, phenomenology, existentialism can be un-Christian when they turn the autonomous subject into an idol, although they can also express the Gospel. Does not the preaching of Jesus about the dignity of all or Paul's view of the Spirit active in each life focus on the free subject? Christianity was not simply the hanging of religious statements on the bulletin boards of minds. From the beginning of his career, Rahner, taught by the previous generation of Jesuits developing a dialogue with modernity, had refused to accept the position of the nineteenth century that a subjective starting point and a transcendental and historical method ran counter to Aquinas. For him the active personality seeks various levels in things, as beings tend to Being, all truths to First Truth.

Theology was an analysis of individuals and communities shot through by history.

Catholic theology needed a positive relationship to modern philosophy; Descartes and Kant were sources to be looked at critically and not just poorly understood enemies to be fought. Modern philosophy, modern theater and music explore the self. Active personalities fashion a world, form a background to all we do, and modernity explores how the active personality fashions a world against which things, whether of economics, science, or religion, exist. Gerald McCool writes of Rahner's "Experiential Thomism":

> His approach to theology had been determined by the nature of the philosophical instrument which he fashioned for himself in *Spirit in the World* and *Hearer of the Word*. That philosophy is authentically Thomistic, but, unlike the Thomism of a previous generation of philosophers and theologians, the focus of its reflections is primarily, almost exclusively, the interior life of the human subject. In the tradition of the existentialist phenomenology that he learned to appreciate through his contact with Heidegger at Freiburg, Rahner's philosophy draws upon the results of a careful discrimination of the various levels of human knowledge and affectivity together with their corresponding objects. . . . His system is, in other words, a philosophical anthropology.[36]

This was a philosophical prelude for letting theology be inspired by the concrete questions of men and women today.[37]

Theology is not eternal and not mathematical. Aware of how our transcendental knowing fashions a background, milieu, and horizon of the colors and sounds of things grasped through the senses, the theologian understands how human beings and societies created a "world" out of the material of nature and life. Maréchal taught him to recognize the creative activity of the subject. Knowing and loving go beyond their objects to an undetermined field of reality, and this dynamism of human life does not follow but goes ahead of knowing this or that object.[38] Transcendental philosophy frees the human subject from being locked up in concepts or propositions. A transcendental method opens up faith through looking at the conditions for revelation coming to the self-understanding of the human person and his or her history. Nevertheless, Rahner is quite clear about the transcendence and initiative of the divine self-communication, that special world of revelation and grace. God is both infinite mystery and a special, intimate presence in our person. The new task for theologians after 1950 is to offer an alternative to the dualism and divine remoteness of textbook theologies after 1840 and 1940.

Heidegger. With other students, Rahner learned in Heidegger's semi-nars to read texts so as to let them disclose their meanings and connections.

> Insofar as it is philosophical, my theology does not really show the systematic and thematic influence of Heidegger. What he communicated was the desire to think, the ability to think. . . . Martin Heidegger was the only teacher for whom I developed the respect that a disciple has for a great master. That had little to do with individual questions or individual formulations of my theology. . . . I really have to doubt whether the truly theological subject matter and work are very much influenced by Heidegger and dependent upon him.[39]

Heidegger and Rahner have a similar point of departure: the one pursues Being, the other pursues divine grace in existential and historical dynamics, in a world and history that are partly mysteries. Broad influences from Martin Heidegger can be seen in the thought of Rahner: the phenomenological, the existential, and the historical. Heidegger's development of "existentials" offered a new framework for locating the free and divine gift of a graced life in the person. In a new style of doing philosophy, the existentials were philosophical and personal aspects of my individual, personal existence. Time, too, was viewed in a new way; it was not just chronological time but existential temporality and historicity. Time and human consciousness let the world appear.

Is there a resemblance in thought-form between Being-in-time and God's self-sharing in history? "In this way he developed an important philosophy of Being. That can and will always have a fascinating significance for a Catholic theologian, for whom God remains the inexpressible Mystery."[40] Rahner's view of salvation history recalls this disclosure motif to explain the unfolding, evolutionary revelation, guided by God, recorded in the Scriptures. Just as the human being projects and lives in a world, a network of interests and involvements, political and artistic and economic milieus influencing us, so Rahner would use that meaning for the world entered into by the Logos, the world of salvation histories, the world of grace. Different cultural and theological epochs emerged in history, because an incarnational revelation disclosed itself in the forms of an age. Christian revelation in a salvation history, the long history of church institutions, and upheaval of change surrounding Vatican II made the theologian's idea of disclosure much less static and momentary than Heidegger's. A few perspectives had been drawn from modern philosophy to present the work of the Word and the Spirit anew.

Aquinas, Kant, Heidegger—three thinkers useful to theology. What they are describing is the dynamic orientation of our knowing and loving outwards, the human person open toward God within corporeality, history, freedom, and language.[41]

Philosophical, patristic, spiritual, and pastoral sources contributed to a theology in a new key as Rahner became a master of information about the church and its traditions and labored to make it again relevant. The distinction between religious things and the transcendental depth of God's presence is a perduring dynamic in Jesus' preaching as he draws people away from rules and numbers to a new way of seeing and living. Paul sees the disciple of the Spirit taking on a new being, a new way of existing. Rahner's theology only uses a few thought-forms and words from several modern philosophies.

> Rahner's theology has no direct philosophical claim but rather moves ever more deeply into theology itself—and yet philosophy is of a considerable importance. I think for example on statements about theological anthropology or the relationship of truth and institution, aspects significant for theology but also ideas opening up the reality of the human person from within non-theological efforts.[42]

There can be no double truth between science and faith; nor can there be a Christian philosophy that sets aside faith while engaging in logical struggles. Philosophies of religions are no real substitute for revelation and traditional theology. The movement of theology through medieval and modern theologies does not reject either side, nor does the church, with creeds and Scripture, fear a variety of philosophies and theologies as the history of the church and dogma show.[43]

III. A THEOLOGIAN'S JOURNEY

As he gave talks and wrote articles, as European history changed and the renewal of the Catholic Church began in the twentieth century, did Karl Rahner's theology assume new approaches? Were there shifts in emphasis or topics? There is a lasting style coming from his Catholic and Jesuit perspective, although there is, too, a wider breadth of consideration and a radicalization in responding to new issues. During Rahner's life and years of teaching, the world changed in many ways. His early philosophical observations in *Geist in Welt* and *Hörer des Wortes* come from a member of a numerous and talented generation of Catholics like J. B. Lotz, Gustav Siewerth, Max Müller, and Bernhard Welte who broke through the confines of neo-Scholastic textbooks to bring basic insights and principles of Thomas into a confrontation with Kant, Scheler, and Heidegger. In terms of theological content, Lehmann noticed how Rahner's early works treated classical problems of philosophy and theology, and then in a middle period applied basic themes to a broader range of topics, while the third phase saw an emphasis upon issues where the transcendental depth of grace enlivened all manner of religious and church forms.[44]

Experts see three periods unfolding in Rahner's theology: (1) a period joining neo-Scholasticism and neo-Kantianism in a philosophy of the self-transcending subject, and then a bridge-period of a philosophy of religion noting how revelation and grace come into an active, free, historical subject leading to the properly theological considerations of person and grace; (2) a period when these seminal approaches enable a creative theological consideration of many topics ranging from nonbelief to sacraments; (3) a period stimulated by Vatican II where countless talks and essays flow from a dialectic that is less nature and grace and more faith and institution, or grace and history. These end with a theological perspective that takes into account the length of history and the breadth of the religious condition of the world (the varied essays enable the appearance of a system in the late 1960s, *Foundations of Christian Faith*); (4) a final period marked by some criticism of church leadership, by an awareness of a decline in European Catholicism, but also by a creative view of church forms, an affirmation of liberating political themes drawn from the gospel, and by essays on grace in the long history of humanity and the church. For Karl Neufeld, a time marked by philosophical frameworks after the beginning of World War II yielded to reflection on the contemporary life of faith in the church from broader perspectives.[45] A focus on Scripture and on human freedom, on the length of human history, and on the extent of human religions led him to see that the new could and must emerge within the church. The world's origin and the world-church are signs of a genuinely historical world and of a God lovingly involved in the time of the human family.

Leo O'Donovan noticed the shift in Rahner's theology from the existential self to the transcendental self in the midst of history. "Clearly it is inadequate to characterize Rahner simply as a transcendental theologian . . . [for] existential structure is always essential related to historical embodiment. . . . Rahner's concern is not merely the abiding, essential truth but rather truth discovered in a historical world of grace."[46] In the final period emerging after 1976, his writings find a global frame of reference as well as a critical and creative focus upon the Catholic Church. There is a "sacramental dialectic" that holds together the reality of Christ and the church in the midst of human religions.[47] Salvation history is anchored in the event of Calvary, although its influence before and after, around and outward, is broad. Building upon a deeper and richer analysis of person and an appreciation of the long diversity of human religious history, there is a directness in approach and a marked creativity. The church—a church for all peoples and not just for Europe—expects a long future in which it serves "'the primordial baptism' of the world"[48] as a gift of "a universal pneumatology."[49] Ecumenism with Protestants, liberation theologies, expanding church structures, and dialogue with the world religions call forth new ideas.

While Jesus had not constituted the church a democracy, the Pauline theology of the universality of charisms and ministries implies that they will have not only activity but voice and influence. For O'Donovan,

> there is something uncanny about these late writings with their bold profession of Christian faith and recognition of its practical perplexities, their staunch support of ecclesial Christianity along with sometimes even angry criticism of its institutional dimensions, their confidence about human possibilities for the future coupled with sober estimation of how much real progress any age can achieve. Beethoven's last quartets come to mind, with their subdued majesty.[50]

Time is present in an individual's existence and in the long history of the human family. The church, source of sacraments, is a communion of realities that await liberation and unfolding. For Johann Baptist Metz, Rahner's thought points to the "theological honor of the human person," a creature to whom revelation has been given and of whom theological thinking is expected.[51] After the 1960s, Rahner became locally critical but globally optimistic, more creative and also more pastoral.

NOTES

1. "Karl Rahner, Zeitgenosse," *GB* 13.
2. Karl Lehmann, "Einführung," *LGG* 6; "Karl Rahner bore for the church a great burden. For over half a century he worked in a responsible and original way to renew theology . . . for all Christians" ("Karl Rahner. Exemplarishe Kraft des theologischen Denkens," in S. Pauly, ed., *Theologen unserer Zeit* [Stuttgart: Kohlhammer, 1997]); see Lehmann, "Introduction," *The Content of the Faith* (New York: Crossroad, 1992) 1–42; "Karl Rahner's Bedeutung für die Kirche," *Stimmen der Zeit* 129 (2004) 3–16. A recent study on the importance of Rahner's theological approach passing through forms of fundamental theology is Winfried Werner, *Fundamentaltheologie bei Karl Rahner. Denkwege und Paradigmen* (Tübingen: Francke, 2004).
3. John Galvin, "Grace for a New Generation," *Commonweal* 112 (January 25, 1985) 40.
4. Herbert Vorgrimler, "Gotteserfahrung im Alltag," in *LGG* 63. Bibliographies list over 1,200 books and articles and give a number of 2,000 works when new editions and translations are counted. One estimate is that Rahner's writings have sold

over 700,000 copies; his edition of the texts of Vatican II with commentary has sold over 100,000 copies.

5. Karl Lehmann, "Karl Rahner und die praktische Theologie," *Zeitschrift für Theologie und Kirche* 126 (2004) 3–15.

6. For information on Rahner's life see *VKR, DKW,* and *IR.*

7. Karl Rahner, *IR* 28. Neufeld, *Die Brüder Rahner* (Freiburg: Herder, 1994) 253; Robert Krieg, *Romano Guardini. A Precursor of Vatican II* (Notre Dame: University of Notre Dame, 1997). Around 1921, the Rahner home hosted a young Italian, son of the owner of a newspaper in Turin, as a kind of exchange student. Giorgio Frassati, athlete, student, hiker, member of the Dominican Laity, was already engaged in combating fascism and in taking care of the seriously sick. He died of polio three years after his time with the Rahners that Karl recalled as a time not of displays of piety but of arguments over soccer games ending in wrestling matches (Rahner, *IR* 33). Frassati was beatified in 1990.

8. "Laudatio auf Erich Przywara," *Gnade als Freiheit* (Freiburg: Herder, 1968) 268; see Thomas O'Meara, *Erich Przywara. His Thought and His Times* (Notre Dame: University of Notre Dame Press, 2002).

9. Rahner, *IR* 42. Delp said at the end of his life that he hoped the Society would become creatively renewed and that Rahner would be the theological source for that (Delp, "Reflexionen über die Zukunft," *Gesammelte Werke* 4 [Frankfurt/Main: Knecht, 1982] 326). On the time of World War II see Vorgrimler, *Gotteserfahrung in Leben und Denken* (Darmstadt: Primus, 2004) 54–9; Rahner looks back at the Third Reich in, "Die Treue zum Gewissen: Die Opfer der 'Weissen Rose,'" *Gnade als Freiheit,* 274–8 and *IR* 39–49.

10. *KRD* 337. "Whether the truly theological subject matter and enterprise [in my work] is very much influenced by Heidegger and dependent upon him I really have to doubt" (*KRD* 13). On Rahner and philosophy see Lehmann's "Karl Rahner: A Portrait," *Content of Faith,* 1–44; "Philosophisches Denken im Werk Karl Rahners," in A. Raffelt, ed., *Karl Rahner in Erinnerung* (Düsseldorf: Patmos, 1994) 10–27.

11. J. B. Lotz, "Im Gespräch," in Günther Neske, ed., *Erinnerung an Martin Heidegger* (Pfullingen: Neske, 1977) 154–61 (English translation in *Philosophy & Theology* 18 [2006]). The Rahner Archive in Innsbruck has a copy of the student summaries by Rahner from a seminar on Heidegger's *Was ist Metaphysik* from 1936-7. Some protocols for Heidegger's seminars written by Karl Rahner are in the same Rahner Archive or at the Heidegger Archive in Marbach.

12. *IR* 42. "Should he simply confess that he is thankful that while having many good schoolmasters of instruction, he had only one whom he can honor as his *teacher*—Martin Heidegger" ("Karl Rahner" in Richard Wisser, ed., *Martin Heidegger im Gespräch* [Munich: Albert, 1970] 48); see Jack Arthur Bonsor, *Rahner, Heidegger and Truth* (Lanham, MD: University Press of America, 1987).

13. Andreas Batlogg, "Karl Rahners theologische Dissertation 'E Latere Christi,'" *Zeitschrift für katholische Theologie* 126 (2004) 111–30.

14. Francis Fiorenza, "Introduction. Karl Rahner and the Kantian Problematic," in Rahner, *Spirit in the World* (New York: Herder and Herder, 1968) xlv; see there the presentation of the historical context of Rahner's dissertation and its views of Kant and Joseph Maréchal as well as early admirers and critics of the book.

15. See *VKR* 67–9, *KRD* 192, *SKR* 148–58, and A. Röper, *Karl Rahner als Seelsorger* (Innsbruck: Tyrolia, 1987).

16. Daniel T. Pekarske has produced a volume of abstractions of all the essays in twenty-three volumes of *Theological Investigations* as a special issue of *Philosophy & Theology* 14 (2002): each essay is located in its volume with references to previous drafts and publications, related to basic theological themes, and summarized. In the 1950s, Hans Urs von Balthasar would refer to the first volume of the *Schriften* as "perhaps the most profound and insightful interpretation of recent scholasticism" (*Zeitschrift für katholische Theologie* 63 [1939] 375). "I consider Karl Rahner to be, on the whole, the strongest theological power of our time" ("Geist und Feuer. Ein Gespräch mit Hans Urs von Balthasar," *Herder Korrespondenz* 30 [1976] 75). In 1978 he rightly saw the point of departure of Rahner's theology to be the broad salvific will of God, its center a christology as a facet of graced anthropology, and its guiding milieu of pastoral Christian life ("Current Trends in Catholic Theology," *Communio* 5 [1978] 79). Yet in the 1980s the anxieties of the earlier *Cordula, oder der Ernstfall* (Einsiedeln: Johannes, 1968) became the dominant mentality, fearing that Rahner's theology, if not unorthodox in its principles or conclusions, held potential unbalance and misdirection.

17. See Robert Kress, *A Rahner Handbook* (Atlanta: John Knox, 1982) 11; on Rahner's contribution to reference works see *VKR* 76–88 and Fahey, "Presidential Address," 90–4.

18. *VKR* 56.

19. *IR* 63.

20. Franz Kardinal König, "Der Konzilstheologe," in *KRB* 62. "In May 1963 the Jesuit General told Rahner that in the future, he would choose Rahner's censors, as before. With this the Holy Office retreated, and from then on until his death Rahner was spared further canonical penalties" (*VKR* 44).

21. *KRD* 262.

22. *VKR* 182. The volume of essays (nine hundred pages) honoring Rahner's eightieth birthday, *Glaube im Prozess,* is arranged around the theme of Rahner and Vatican II; see, too, G. Wassilowsky, *Universales Heilssakrament Kirche. Karl Rahners Beitrag zur Ekklesiologie des II. Vatikanums* (Innsbruck: Tyrolia, 2001).

23. At a celebratory conference he spoke of the forces at work in Guardini's era and about the priest's influence upon young people in the years after the First World War. He mentioned the books and lectures setting forth not theories on the philosophy of religion but great artists and thinkers, the poetry and painting of Dante and Rembrandt. "In these interpretations Guardini brought his thinking through differentiation and assimilation to meet a large part of the tradition of the Western Spirit. He saw himself working at 'the end of the modern age', in a time of transition, at the edge of a barren and hard time without any Muses. Still, the past would remain vital, unburdening itself of its contributions for our future" (Rahner, "Festvortrag," in Karl Foster, ed., *Akademische Feier zum 80. Geburtstag von Romano Guardini* [Würzburg: Echter, 1965] 23).

24. See Roman Siebenrock, "Erfahrungen im Karl-Rahner-Archiv," *Stimmen der Zeit* 129 (2004) 36–41; Daniel Deckers, "Der gemeinsame Weg mit Karl Rahner— der Assistent (1964–1968)," *Der Kardinal, Karl Lehmann. Eine Biographie* (Munich:

32   *God in the World: A Guide to Karl Rahner's Theology*

Pattloch, 2002) 124–8; Dorothea Sattler, "Zeugnis im Immanenten für den Tran-
szendenten. Spuren einer Verwandtschaft im Denken von Karl Lehmann und Karl
Rahner," in Albert Raffelt, ed., *Weg und Weite* (Freiburg: Herder, 2001) 403–18.

    25. *IR* 75.

    26. "Erfahrungen eines katholischen Theologen," in *GGM* 105–19; "Experi-
ences of a Catholic Theologian," *TS* (2000) 61, 3–15.

    27. William Dych, *Karl Rahner* (Collegeville: Liturgical Press, 1992) 14f.

    28. See Robert Kress, "Sources of Rahner's Theology," *A Rahner Handbook*, ch.
3, and the writings of Harvey Egan, Andreas Batlogg, and Karl Neufeld.

    29. See "Philosophy and Philosophizing," *TI* 9, 58–63.

    30. *Summa Theologiae* I, q. 6, a. 4; q. 12, a. 13; q. 23, a. 1; q. 26, a. 4; q. 43; "The
New Law is principally the grace of the Holy Spirit" *Summa Theologiae* I–II, q. 106,
a. 1.

    31. "And between these two movements [of the soul toward the mental image]
there is this difference. The first movement by which one is moved to the image as
it is of some thing differs from the movement which is toward the reality. But the
second movement which is towards the image as an image is one and the same with
that which is toward the reality" (*Summa Theologiae* III, 25, 3); see *KRD* 11–18
and Gerald McCool, "Karl Rahner and the Christian Philosophy of St. Thomas
Aquinas," in William J. Kelly, ed., *Theology and Discovery: Essays in Honor of Karl
Rahner, s.j.* (Marquette, WI: Marquette University Press, 1980) 63–93.

    32. *Summa Theologiae* III, qq. 6; 7.

    33. "Thomas Aquinas, Patron of Theological Studies," *The Great Church Year.
The Best of Karl Rahner's Homilies, Sermons, and Meditations* (New York: Crossroad,
1993) 317. On Aquinas treating God seeking through being and grace to contact in
various ways the finite human person, see "An Investigation of the Incomprehensi-
bility of God in St. Thomas Aquinas," *TI* 12, 248f.

    34. Like Aquinas, Rahner emphasized a single, intrinsic supernatural dynamic in
revelation and grace as well as a divine efficacy (even in the labyrinth of human religions). His transcendental and existential approach sets aside the Baroque emphases
upon co-operation, upon distinctions between natural and supernatural virtues, and
a separation in the Christian's life between asceticism and mysticism. The infused
virtues are not transitory powers for good deeds but God-given potentialities to
transcend oneself toward the immediacy of God and express the working out of an
authentic act of freedom through the freeing grace of God ("The Christian Understanding of Redemption," *TI* 21, 241). The arrival of this theology (along with that of
Henri de Lubac and Pierre Teilhard de Chardin) seems to coincide with the decline
of the neo-Scholasticism of Molina and Suarez in the Society of Jesus. "Grace has
always been given, and this supernatural formal object is always at work somewhere
in the totality of human consciousness. There has never been a time or a place that
was not a part of the history of revelation. . . . I am at this point being radically
Thomistic, and I stand quite apart from the typical Jesuit line of thought" (*FW* 48).

    35. "The Importance of Thomas Aquinas," *FW* 45. "I believe my dissertation in
philosophy can to an extent indicate how my generation viewed its relationship to
Thomas. This relation differed from that of the classical Thomists, especially that of
the Dominicans. For them Thomas's writings were something like a second Scrip-

ture upon which one was supposed to comment. . . . I by no means want to deny that this sort of contact with Thomas was important. But Thomas was read by my generation as a great father of the church. This was certainly true of Max Müller, Johannes B. Lotz, Gustav Siewerth, and even of Erich Przywara who exercised an important influence on the generation before me, an influence which found expression not so much in individual doctrines as in a particular style of thinking" (Ibid.).

36. McCool, *The Theology of Karl Rahner* (Albany, NY: Magi Books, 1961) 31f.; see McCool, "Karl Rahner and the Christian Philosophy of Saint Thomas Aquinas," 187; Otto Muck, *The Transcendental Method* (New York: Herder & Herder, 1968); "Karl Rahner als Philosoph," in Emil Coreth, et al., eds., *Christliche Philosophie im katholischen Denken des 19. und 20. Jahrhunderts,* 2 (Graz: Styria, 1988) 600–8.

37. KRD 324. There may be a little influence on Rahner from Catholic theologians of the first half of the nineteenth century. The subtitle of Rahner's *Foundations* includes *"Begriff,"* and the work refers in opening pages to F. A. Staudenmaier, student of the Schellingian J. S. Drey and a romantic idealist theologian at Tübingen and Freiburg. For the first third of the nineteenth century, Catholics without any suspicion of heterodoxy fashioned large systems beginning with a transcendental analysis of the human subject's powers (see Thomas O'Meara, *Romantic Idealism and Roman Catholicism. Schelling and the Theologians* [Notre Dame: University of Notre Dame Press, 1982]).

38. DKR 70–3.

39. KRD 257.

40. IR 45. There may be also an influence of Heidegger in terms of time not only in existential temporality but in the historical variety of church forms and ideas. If truth is a disclosure process of aspects of Being, salvation history could be understood as an expanded form of the history of Being in the realm of grace. "The presumed relationship between Heidegger and Rahner does not imply that Rahner's theology is derived from Heidegger's philosophy, but points out a spiritual affinity as well as a similar method and way of thinking. Rahner's affinity to Heidegger appears clearly in an early Innsbruck seminar on 'mystery.' . . . The Mystery of God, though constantly evading, is yet appearing, by opening a space for its apparition in the apex of the human being which could be called our 'transcendence' or 'ecstasis.' . . . In addition Rahner's indebtedness to Heidegger breathes through his new reception as well as synthetic translation of the church's mystical tradition, which lies at the very base of his theology" (Klaus P. Fischer, "Philosophie und Mystagogie. Karl Rahners 'reduction in mysterium' als Prinzip seines Denkens," *Zeitschrift für Katholische Theologie* 120 [1998] 56).

41. Marek Chojnacki, *Die Nähe des Unbegreifbaren. Der moderne philosophische Kontext der Theologie Karl Rahners und seine Konsequenzen in dieser Theologie* (Fribourg: Universitätsverlag, 1996) 98ff.

42. Karl Lehmann, "Philosophisches Denken im Werk Karl Rahners," in A. Raffelt, ed., *Karl Rahner in Erinnerung* (Düsseldorf: Patmos, 1994) 11. For a presentation of a possible influence from Maurice Blondel in terms of a new apologetics and the intrinsic nature of grace, see A. Raffelt, H. Verweyen, *Karl Rahner* (Munich: Beck, 1997) 20, 40; and Albert Raffelt, "Rahner und Blondel," in A. Batlogg et al., *Was den Glauben in Bewegung bringt* (Freiburg: Herder, 2004) 17–32.

43. "Philosophy and Theology," *SM* 5, 20–4; see "Theological Observations on the Concept of Time," *TI* 11, 288–308.

44. In the final period there was a new interpretation of the history of revelation, one bringing together the history of the world and the history of grace. This had creative and influential implications in sacrament and church and in how the history of religions leads to Jesus and how lengthy human history is touched by God (Lehmann, "Introduction," *The Content of Faith,* 33); see Roman Siebenrock, "'Draw nigh to God and He will draw nigh to you' (James 4:8): The Development of Karl Rahner's Theological Thinking in Its First Period," *Louvain Studies* 29 (2004) 28–48. Rahner was consistent, remaining engaged by and faithful to the renewal of the Catholic Church, its new openness to dialogue, the vitality and pluralism of theologies, and the courage to entertain the issues of the time. There is nothing of the anxious step backward after 1970 marking theologians who were frightened by the postconciliar period like Hans Urs von Balthasar, Joseph Ratzinger, Henri de Lubac, or Avery Dulles.

45. Neufeld, "La relation entre philosophie et théologie selon K. Rahner," *Pour une philosophie chrétienne. philosophie et théologie* (Paris: Lethielleux-Le Sycamore, 1983) 85–108.

46. O'Donovan, "A Journey into Time: The Legacy of Karl Rahner's Last Years," *TS* 46 (1985) 644. Yves Tourenne has written a study on the "later Rahner," concluding that the fifteen years after 1970 manifest "an openness to pluralism in general and to the totality of the real . . . , the catholicity of a theological work." Characteristics of permanence, development, and radicalization mark his path as he changes and remains the same, offers the same format for new and varied issues (*La Théologie du dernier Rahner* [Paris: Cerf, 1995] 16, 31, 329).

47. "A Final Harvest: Karl Rahner's Last Theological Writings," *Religious Studies Review* 11 (1985) 357–9; see O'Donovan, "A Journey into Time. The Legacy of Karl Rahner's Last Years," *TS* 46 (1985) 645. Heinrich Fries spoke of Rahner's "Kairos," a historical moment bursting with new ideas, risking an inquiry into the demands of the Christ as personal and universal and passing beyond frozen philosophy and automatic grace. "Der Anonyme Christ—Das Anonyme Christentum als Kategorien christlichen Denkens," in Elmar Klinger, ed., *Christentum innerhalb und ausserhalb der Kirche* (Freiburg: Herder, 1976) 25.

48. "The Church's Redemptive Historical Provenance from the Death and Resurrection of Jesus," *TI* 19, 32.

49. "Reflections on *Foundations of the Christian Faith*," *Theological Digest* 28 (1980) 211. Richard Lennan's *The Ecclesiology of Karl Rahner* (Oxford: Oxford University Press, 1995) explores the ecclesiological emphases of the early and later Rahner.

50. "A Final Harvest: Karl Rahner's Last Theological Writings," 357.

51. "Karl Rahners Ringen um die theologische Ehre des Menschen," A. Raffelt, ed., *Karl Rahner in Erinnerung* (Düsseldorf: Patmos, 1994) 70f.

Chapter 3

Fashioning a Theology for Today

"For a Christian, Christian existence is ultimately the totality of existence. This totality opens out into the dark abysses of the wilderness we call God. . . . There must always be new attempts to reflect upon the single whole of Christianity."[1] Rahner wanted to make what was most basic in Christianity attractive and intelligible to people living today. Albert Görres explored this effort:

> What makes Rahner's theology different from other theologies? It seems to be that he develops a special way of thinking along with others. He tries to penetrate deeply into the perspective of others, to understand why an atheist, Communist, natural scientist, psychiatrist or any other person thinks the way they do, and why they feel the way they feel. . . . Rahner found consoling and helping words for countless minds that were confused and for hearts that were wounded. He opened and made attractive a way that had been closed for legions of people injured by the church and disappointed by God; he found access to God once lost, access to a creation full of terrors; he found a way to a bloody history, to a suffering Gospel, to a burdened church.[2]

Is, however, this expression of Jesus' teaching difficult to understand? Is it a too inclusive and optimistic Christian liberalism? Is it a Germanic theology tainted by the philosophical language of Kant or Heidegger? Is his thought a modern philosophy of religion? Rahner's theology is direct and clear, original but consistent. A brief meditation on courage in daily life or a creative essay on the intelligibility of the phrase "hypostatic union"—both hold a similar manner of thinking. Important thinkers may produce many volumes, but their insights, no matter how enlightening and influential, are not many, and their perspectives are the ways by which they engage the world. Rahner's expressions and insights draw faith in Jesus' teaching into contemporary thought-forms. Is Rahner worth pursuing and learning from? Andrew Tallon writes: "'The greatest Catholic theologian of the twentieth century'—for nearly fifty years this is how we have been describing Karl Rahner. Today his reputation is more solid than ever. . . . There is every indication that a foundation in Rahner will be the ticket to theology's agenda for the twenty-first century."[3]

I. A THEOLOGY FOR TODAY: FIVE CHALLENGING ISSUES

Rahner, as he often said, became a Jesuit and theologian to announce the good news of Jesus' teaching, and no matter how distinguished his academic career appeared, that activity remained his vocation.

> I think that in all human experiences of individual realities limitation is ultimately experienced along with that reality [of grace]. . . . All that touches a human being ultimately displays an inability to fulfill the total capacity of the human being. . . . Christianity, however, preaches an absolute joy, an absolute future, an unlimited reality—and this is what it means to be, absolutely, "Good News."[4]

Johann Baptist Metz observes, "Rahner's theology is not stimulated by a traditional canon of old questions leading to a system. His theology has a canon but it is a cluster of life's questions, questions that are not comfortable ones but clamoring unpleasant questions examined carefully."[5] A creative and sometimes scholarly look at the profound realities of the Christian faith has the goal of serving the ordinary Christian concerned with life.

Rahner, through his studies, knew well patristic and medieval theologies (and the dominant neo-Scholasticism of the 1940s and 1950s); he insisted that theology has to do with God's revelation as it passes through the filters of human life and consciousness. His writings stand in contrast to some Protestant and Catholic theologies of the late twentieth century that never get beyond sketching a method or a hermeneutic, and that end not with insights into the workings of God but with the creation of novel terms. Theology should always be treating some subject matter, some form, some object, some aspect of revelation. If Rahner does not reduce theology to methodology, he also does not (as is done in ecclesiastical circles) compose a theology apart from society and people.⁶ Whatever you call faith, it must entertain and speak of realities and of radical immediacy to God. Words like "revelation" and "salvation" need to escape immature stories and pictures in the confines of a fundamentalism. Translating dogmatic theology into the pastoral life of the church and into theological education occurs at various levels. Rahner's work, born of a particular historical moment of the church and of theology, involved a move from a universally imposed Scholastic theology (in sparse Aristotelian metaphysics) into a pluralism of theological plans, but without diminishing faith or church. A knowledge of the early church, insight into Thomas Aquinas, and knowledge of the Baroque and neo-Scholastic periods prepare for new perspectives on Christian life. This particular age in the journey of Catholicism began sixty years ago and more, and much still lies ahead of the church rediscovering its full reality.

Five issues stand out. Those five issues influenced and challenged Rahner during the decades of his work, and their continuing presence today explains his contemporary import, because in these areas his thought remains indispensable.

The *first* is the search for a modern Catholic theology, a theology accepting the person and history as important. A few Catholics had sought a theology that was not neo-medieval during the time of Romantic Idealism; in the first third of the nineteenth century, some had fashioned theologies of self and community in development (later they would be influential at Vatican II). Vatican authority condemned efforts to fashion theology in a modern form and sought to impose an eternal (medieval) theology with a perennial (Aristotelian) format. Could Catholic Christianity express a real and historical revelation in the forms of the modern philosophies of self, freedom, and time? Rahner's theology showed that it could be done.

> Rahner went beyond the alternative of simply continuing an exhausted neo-scholasticism and seized upon impulses of modern thinking which were viewed as hostile to faith. . . . His thought made it possible for theology faithful to the church to use positively principles of modern thinking and exegesis while remaining true to tradition and the classical teachings of the church. Rahner was a bridge builder from neo-scholasticism to contemporary theology.⁷

The *second* issue is that of the human person living amid grace and revelation, and sin. Theologies from the sixteenth to the twentieth centuries usually expressed revelation as a set of propositions; catechisms and seminary textbooks set forth biblical truth in sentences whose terminology and conceptuality were that of Greek metaphysics. Grace, life in the Spirit, became transitory flashes of divine power touching the mental faculties of human nature described in Greek metaphysics. The Catholic Church resembled an electric company where actual graces were gingerly dispatched to human beings—usually Roman Catholics—summoned by human prayers and rituals. Theologies of grace as a divine personal love or as a life given at baptism were marginalized although they were not lost. Sins occurred when individuals enacted the bad actions listed in a casuistic catalogue, while original sin with its consequent addictions and habits and social evil was neglected. A neutral human person lived between flashes of grace and kinds of sin. Rahner did not relativize sin or secularize grace, but in a reversal he emphasized their depth: grace as the trinitarian presence and sin as an atmosphere of evil.

Third, in the course of the twentieth century, Europeans witnessed great numbers of intellectuals and workers leaving the church for progressive social and political movements. They sought a more humane society, justice against entrenched and selfish establishments (including the church's hierarchy). Catholics had to ponder the modern European who, leaving the church, sought at that time at great personal cost the improvement of the men and women around him.[8] In the Christian view, did not a life of sacrifice for others require grace? How did grace draw forward those who worked for social justice (a theme of modern literature)?

A new experience of earth as a global village in the 1960s, with people caught up in their religions, placed demands on a theology of grace within the human family. This was a *fourth* challenge. Jet travel and electronic communications were joining the world. The traveler—a tourist or a CEO—saw firsthand that the devotees of other religions were not lost in superstition. They, too, sought grace and hope and faith. How was grace touching them? If there were no salvation outside of Christianity (and Catholic theologies had taught that there was), why had God created billions of people who could not possibly know of Jesus? Rahner drew the reality of a saving history directed by a loving God through the Spirit of Christ into this tumultuous global collection of religions.

A *fifth* theological area of import was the history of the church's worship and social structure. Little had changed in the Catholic Church from the sixteenth century (even from the thirteenth century) up to the renewal of the 1960s. Vatican II reformulated anew the rites of the sacraments and offered new theologies of sacramental life to replace the simple seminary manuals and children's catechisms. How should one explain what was basic in revelation and grace both as a rich but mysterious divine presence in history and also as a source of changing forms in Christian life? Rahner was a master at showing how different cultural forms through the centuries could present a single religious reality: for instance, the same sacrament assumed different rites for different peoples, or the Bishop of Rome had a public role in the fourth century that was different from that in the nineteenth. This was important because Catholicism around the world was passing beyond the fixed monopoly of Latin phrases and late Baroque forms as it sought to be more than European.

These five topics, appearing as a constellation in the 1960s, are not academic exercises but issues in faith and church. Liberal Protestantism, so dominant from 1860 to 1960, eventually faded because it explained away the reality and history of sacrament and dogma: it exchanged realities for theories, replacing the supernatural with the psychological and disdained any concrete form for faith. Rahner was a quintessentially Catholic theologian. He did not diminish the analogous realities of Jesus Christ, the Eucharist, or the Christian. At the same time he enjoyed distinguishing between what is the basic Christian message and what are later expressions and forms.

While the Jesuit spontaneously and maturely thought somewhat out of the language of modern German philosophy, he is not much concerned with philosophy for its own sake. "I am no scholar. In this work of theology, I only want to be a man, a Christian, and, as much as possible, a priest of the church. Perhaps a theologian cannot desire anything else. In any case, the science of theology, as such, was never important to me."[9] His background in Ignatian spirituality and in existential philosophy gave him a personal and pastoral direction, while his experience of a church embattled during the Nazi period or engaged with church change after Vatican II gave his ideas a realism. He wrote often on the challenges to theology and on the theology of the future, a theology that would be pluralistic, ecumenical, engaged with science and with new social structure, a theology whose fidelity to the Gospel included taking the human person and the length of salvation history seriously.[10] His perspective is modern, indeed, late-modern in that it is global, historical, cosmic, traditional. Essays in books in his honor illustrate his importance around the world, an inspiration for theologies in Asian and Latin America.[11] Karl Lehmann wrote on the tenth anniversary of Rahner's death:

> In church and society, he stands as a vital figure for today. When we read him—now at a certain distance—he seems often to stand closer to our present situation than to his own in an earlier time. There is a view of the church today in many of his writings from various decades which has prophetic, even visionary elements, which can help us in our situation.

. . . Karl Rahner remains an example for theology and for the life of faith.[12]

Rahner offers a traditional and insightful theology of grace in the depth of each person, a view of revelation in the long history of human religions. His theology begins with questioning, with a human search for truth, with an awareness that it alone does not create truth, and that the Truth lies beyond academic study and research.

II. THREE CHARACTERISTICS OF A CONTEMPORARY THEOLOGY

Three characteristics of Rahner's theology are fundamental and recurring. To understand them is to understand his reexpression of Christian revelation. They are: (1) the human person; (2) a mysterious and silent but real presence of God beyond that of creation; (3) history.[13]

The Human Person. As already noted, the modern world—its philosophies and architecture, its theater and science—is marked by the centrality of the human subject. For centuries after the Protestant Reformation and the Enlightenment, emphasis was given to the human person, her psychological depth, his multiplicity of creative activities. With the advent of modern art, the realistic figure yielded to form and color, offering not a picture but an impression, an expression, an abstraction. Science and mathematics moved deeper into minute analyses distant from the realities of nature. From 1850 to 1960 the Catholic Church sought to ignore any move to the subject. Would not that orientation suppress historical revelation or relativize moral principles? Church authority feared democracy and freedom, teaching that there was one perennial perspective: Aristotelian and medieval. That intellectual colonialism—all people had the same way of thinking—was obviously false: the very history of the church showed diversity. A convincing message and a communal liturgy do not come down from heaven in pages written in gold, but emerge out of God at work in people. Jesus' teaching is very much about the human person, a defense of that person against false religion.

What were the forms and powers of the knowing and acting self? Modern philosophers sought in the nineteenth century a description of the subject, an analysis of the self called transcendental ("transcendental" means not something transcendent like God, but the forms of the knowing subject). The transcendental horizon offers an active background in which the knower and the known encounter each other; the knower is a subject with its forms of understanding, and the thing known is an object open to analysis. The person knows about herself and grasps herself only in objects known. Martin Heidegger expanded subjectivity into a presentation of the person as existence-in-the-world, knowing and living amid the disclosures of being and time. Could Catholic theology reflect on faith from the point of view of the person in history and culture? For Rahner, theology begins with the human person, and the church begins with the community it serves.

> How can a Christian speak appropriately of God unless at the same time he also speaks of the human person? The word made flesh is and remains the eternal and unlimited man. We cannot know God as he is without at the same time thinking of him as the God who made the human species. Consequently we cannot have a complete theology without considering its anthropological aspects. If we want to talk of God properly, we have to talk of human beings.[14]

Reflective theology and pastoral ministry begin by inquiring into the subjectual dynamics of people, hearers of the Word.

"World" is a theme of modern philosophy. World is not a collection of buildings or a forest but the milieu of human life. Men and women live in their world and not in the cosmos of Greece or the forum of Rome, not in a medieval cathedral town or a Baroque court. The experiences of a surrounding cultural world (Africa holds worlds distinct from Europe) fashion and express each person. Modern philosophy does not always end in solitary human existence against a stark landscape of nothingness but explores an active depth, a horizon of meanings. An existential and transcendental analysis seeks to understand the human person through a spectrum of approaches ranging from Jungian psychology to political movements; in North America this is found more in psychology and sociology and film.[15] In Christianity, world can mean three things: creation, a sinful world hostile to morality and love, and a world loved by God. The Holy Spirit is also fashioning a world, a world of grace.

> This world has a history which has entered on its eschatological stage through the incarnation, cross and resurrection of the eternal Word of God. The outcome of history in its entirety is already decided by Christ in the depths of reality. . . . The various aspects of this theological, many-sided concept of the world can never be wholly separated from one another.[16]

The longing of the human person, the search of this particular individual—whether in Nairobi or Hong Kong—is never solitary but occurs within the horizon of the surrounding world. God's grace does not disdain but accepts cultural history.

The Jesuit stressed two distinct aspects of the active self.

First, there is a *transcendence* in the sense of the person reaching out toward truth and reality, a self-transcendence. Knowing grasps more than the mind sketches; loves embraces all of the person loved. Implicit knowledge and love may lack the explicit forms and details of what is known and loved and yet hold them in a general way. The human person is always seeking, and that active quest holds at a deep level some contact with a fuller reality. The personality moves toward particular objects and draws them into its world; at the same time, the person with his or her mysterious depth goes beyond the object. This or that thing, with its characteristics and words, is always grasped in a broader, unknown, silent horizon of possible knowing and possible freedom even if it is difficult to describe this horizon. "The movement of the spirit and of freedom, and the horizon of this movement, are boundless. Every object of our conscious mind which we encounter in our social world and environment is merely a stage, a constantly new starting-point in the movement which reaches into the everlasting."[17] Here the seeker and believer may touch "God" or "the future" even when they reject the words. In knowing and freedom, the human person is unavoidably a being of transcendence.

Second, *transcendental* forms influence how a person thinks and loves and acts. The palm tree, the desert, the hot sun in Los Angeles today are similar to the same realities in Egypt at the time of Moses, but the ways men and women understand and employ them are different. To be a Nigerian, to be a woman, to be advanced in age will inevitably illumine the way one senses life and God. Subjective forms can be limiting, and they can also be liberating, dynamic openings to life and grace. Individual knowing is transcendental as it encompasses general, sustaining forms of the individual's knowledge and love.

These background forms fashion a world. Man is not merely a biological or social reality. "Rather his subjectivity and his free, personal self-interpretation take place precisely in and through his being in the world, in time, and in history, or better, in and through world, time and history. The question of salvation cannot be answered by bypassing human historicity and social life."[18]

Because the thought-forms of a place and a time, general modalities of life and understanding, influence what is particular and concrete, they are the place of revelation and grace. In terms of God and the kingdom of God, a transcendental horizon anticipates and points to the religious realm of God's self-communication touching the believer.

What is important is to help the human being understand that there is an entirely different kind of experience, namely a transcendental one. In this experience of spiritual knowing and freedom we are able to know what we call God. This transcendental experience points to God and is also the condition which makes each and every other experience possible.[19]

Transcendental knowledge is the horizon against which the things—trees, clouds, buildings—stand. Things and objects appear in a transcendental background. Its opposite, "categorical knowledge" (in Kant's terminology), is easier to understand: it is knowledge of things and objects, simple and direct, coming through the senses. The pair, categorical and transcendental, suggested to Rahner applications for understanding the reign of God and the presence of the Holy Spirit.[20]

> The infinite horizon, which is the term of transcendence and which opens us to unlimited possibilities of encounter this or that particular thing cannot itself be given a name. . . . This infinite and silent terminal point influences us. It presents itself, however, to us in the mode of stepping back, of silence and distance, so that speaking of it always requires listening to its silence.[21]

The *self-transcendent* quest of the human person—we see it in love, in the arts, in life—points, leads to God active in a *transcendental* way of God being present. The source of grace and revelation seeks to become concrete within an interplay of the human and the divine. The Christian God is not the distant causal machine of the Enlightenment nor a deity who fails to solve the problems of a natural disaster, nor the miracle worker of every fundamentalism. God is intimately present to men and women in a special way, present as the predestining plan and power of life now and in the future.[22]

> The concepts and words which we use to talk of the Eternal and to which we are constantly referred, are not the original actual mode of the reality of that experience of nameless mystery surrounding the island of our everyday awareness but merely the tiny signs and idols we erect and have to erect so that they constantly remind us of the original, unthematic, silently offered and proffered, and graciously silent experience of the difference of the mystery.[23]

God has created human personalities so that they desire the divine and so that they can receive its teaching. "We live in a world which always and everywhere is directed by the secret grace of God towards the eternal life of God: this occurs always and everywhere, whenever a person does not expressly shut himself off by real culpable unbelief from this innermost supernatural, grace-given dynamism of the world."[24] To present Jesus' message of the kingdom of God, Rahner began with the human and not with religious rules, with personal and social life and not with dogmas or rubrics. Human existence is the place of God's presence and the grammar of God's revelation. Gerald McCool explains the influence of early philosophical reflection on a theology:

> Transcendental anthropology and the metaphysical conclusions drawn from its reflection on the intellectual and volitional activity of the incarnate human person constitute one of the most obvious threads of unity running through . . . theological reflections on the graciousness of the supernatural, the dogmatic concepts, the knowability of universal propositions expressing the demands of the natural law, and the need and possibility of a formal existential moral theology. . . . [Their] constant theme is the relation of the free, self-possessing human subject to God and to the world.[25]

Each personality receives God's self-sharing in a transcendental way: that is, God's offer of grace, retaining the sovereignty, freedom, and initiative of God, comes to people first in a transcendental, general, silent mode.

So beyond the idea of God being transcendent there are two modes of human life: self-transcendent, and transcendental. The first refers to the inner psychological orientation of human life to something more; the second points out a general background reality bestowing conditions of things, the world fashioned by culture and language. A transcendental theology is one that begins with the general life of the human subject and presumes, from the perspective of faith, that this active general life of a person is already the place of grace, and that God's loving presence enters and respects the modalities of life. "If, moreover, the horizon of human existence which grounds and encompasses all human knowledge is a mystery, and it is, then man has a positive affinity, given with grace, to those Christian mysteries which constitute the basic content of faith."[26]

God's Gift of Shared Life. The self-transcendence of the human person seeks God. Proofs for God's existence and speculation about God's being have been called a "natural revelation." The God directing the galaxies (whose own world is spirit) cannot be an object of our sense knowledge, of our "categorical" knowledge, eluding circumscription by material things, and, nonetheless, faith holds that God contacts us in subtle ways.

> The unlimited extent of our spirit in knowledge and freedom (ineluctably and unthematically given in every ordinary experience) allows us to experience what is meant by God as the revealing and fulfilling ground of

that expanse of the Spirit and its limitless movement. Transcendental experience, even when and where it is mediated through an actual categorical object, is always divine experience in the midst of everyday life.[27]

Concluding to a cause of the universe, Rahner observed, is not a great step forward in human life for it presents the fact of God more as a question than as an answer; it reveals little.

> Still, this leaves God unknown because God's ultimate relationship with spiritual creatures cannot be known in an unequivocal way by this means. Thus it remains unknown whether God intends (or is able) to be for us the absolute intimacy of radical self-communication, or a silent, self-contained infinity keeping us imprisoned at a distance in our finitude; or further, whether God's response to our sinful rejection of God would be judgment or forgiveness.[28]

God is distant from us, an invisible being, a powerful creator. Is he a being who can be ignored? A force facing with little power the vagaries of human politics and religion? Moreover, we have false images of God deep in our consciousness: the strict parent, the fickle deity, the cold judge. None of this describes the true and living God who is mystery and love. Atheism or depression may simply be letting-go of these dubious theologies of God. Christianity says much more.[29]

Christianity proclaims that there is a true revelation of God.

> It is not simply implicit in the spiritual nature of the human person but exhibits the character of an event; it is dialogic; in it God addresses us, makes known to us not merely what can be deduced at all times and in all places from the necessary reference of all earthly things to God (here precisely the question of God, and the questions which this mystery presents to human beings), but rather all that remains unknown in and for the world even when the world is presupposed: the intimate being of God and God's free, personal relationship with spiritual [knowing, free] creatures.[30]

Revelation is "the self-communication of God," that is, God giving a share in his life to men and women. The German verb *mitteilen* is sometimes translated into English as "communication," but that cerebral term has overtones of the world of media and weakens the notion of shared life. This special divine presence Jesus called the kingdom of God, while theologians call it grace or revelation. God's presence is personal: not in the Greek sense that the Trinity is three Persons, but in the modern sense that God knows and loves each man and woman individually, intimately, profoundly. This divine presence is not derived from human life—it is not an idealist ontology or a contemporary psychology—although it enters into human life. The revelation of God's life is the revelation of us in that life. "Divine self-communication means, then, that God can communicate himself in his own reality to what is not divine without ceasing to be infinite reality and absolute mystery, and without man ceasing to be a finite existent different from God."[31] God's mystery remains even as God's love vitalizes. God's self-sharing emerges in the opening of the letter to the Ephesians and subsequently in theologies from the first centuries of an economy of salvation and divinization of the believer, and it is found, too, in Thomas Aquinas who spoke of a participation or share in the being of the Trinity.

God exists for us as a source of a further plan of life and love for humanity, not as a source of philosophical axioms or miracles. Christianity is not a catechism or a law book, not one correct set of religious rites, not an insurance policy but an access to a real world, divine but invisible, a distinct but intimate Presence.

Rahner spoke often of the "experience" of God. What does this mean? This underlying experience, an experience of depth and context, is not what we mean in English by "experience." That word means a physical and transitory emotion, while transcendental experience is an underlying psychological condition; this is not the experience of enthusiasts or charismatics but an experience of a silent mystery in a real but unthematized knowing.[32] Graced experience enables and flows from a transcendental presence of God; it does not reject human language and the layers of an individual's psychological life but bubbles up through them to influence daily life. Human words and actions always stand as servants of a deeper presence, aware of their limitations. Experience has its own dialectic, moving from my experience to the experience of God more as a presence than an object.

What engages people in religion begins in a transcendental manner. Christian words about revelation and salvation have limits and remind us to look beneath the forms and language of believers and devotees of other religions to grasp what is actually being said. Dogmas are pointers and summaries. The Christian view of God protests against polytheism and pantheism and also against magic and superstition outside and within the churches. To Christians the divine presence beneath their creed and sacraments invites them not to hide or barter but to explore more and more the breadth and depth of "grace." The Christian transcendent God is a God revealing life and holiness and condemning injustice and evil. Born of a universal will of salvation meets the longing of the person and the course of history, God's grace meets the longing of the person and makes history, without fully ending secularity or overcoming its sinfulness. Mature theology begins from the point of departure of a godly God, a divine being who is not an angry judge or a watching failure but a being whose revelation points not to a sectarianism of salvation but to a universality of love in the format of history. Here there is a return to the eschatological, future direction of Christian origins: grace has been reoriented toward salvation, and God's will is powerful, intent on saving all. This, Heribert Mühlen says, the interpretation of God's plan of love in terms of history and eschatology, is "the main concern of Rahner's theology of grace."[33]

History. Time drives human life forward. Time discloses inventions and discoveries. Time moves and leads in salvation history the transcendental presence of grace into the concrete, into words and rituals. The agonizing solitary of existentialist novels and films from 1950 faded, and a person stepped forth, a person who knows that she lives on a planet of networks of politics and communications, lives amid a lengthy history of religions, lives in liturgies and spiritualities. Catholic theology after the 1960s and 1970s became increasingly historical, less neo-Scholastic; and then, less existential and more multicultural and global. Time flowing through the person and through societies and cultures with their arts and sciences is what we call history. The human person lives not in a static now but in an ever-moving line of change, the recipient of grace loose in the world. Anne Carr writes: "Transcendence, for Rahner, is always transcendence in history, or history as transcendent. This dual structure implies a dual method: an examination of *both* the essential human structures implied in Christian revelation and examination of the historical, concrete data of Christian revelation itself."[34] God's presence does not simply tolerate his creature, time, but employs history as a means for unfolding the divine plan and life. God enters history, the movement of God's presence through human religion, and the Jewish covenant leads to Jesus Christ. "Emmanuel," "the Word made flesh," tells of God's plan to become tangible in history as the Word pitches its tent in the journey of humanity. Incarnation means not only Jesus of Nazareth but all the moments and people and ways in which grace is realized over a million years. Grace pervades each existential person and, consequently, each age.[35]

History in Rahner's theology refers to several themes: the individual's story, God and change, the history of salvation, the history of religion, and the history of the church's forms. The history of salvation is coterminous with the entire history of humanity open to grace. Salvation is salvation history; revelation speaks during centuries through mystics and prophets and theologians. God offers an intimacy that also is infinite distance, and in a dynamic of incarnation in Jesus and in all men and women now and in the future.[36] Grace flowing from and to Jesus aims at the future.

History is not even and smooth: there are moments and times of graced intensification—Abraham's call, the Exodus, the emergence of Hebrew prophets, the birth of Jesus of Nazareth. Rahner offers a theory of the history of salvation on a broad scale. He goes on to ponder how Christian forms of theology, liturgy, and spirituality find different cultural realizations; for instance, how the forgiveness of sins or episcopal leadership assume through twenty centuries different forms. In Rahner's theology, existential subjectivity and historicity are the place of grace. "The history of salvation, therefore, is history *on God's part.*"[37]

Human Person, Divine Life, Terrestrial History—these three characteristics just mentioned give a structure to the synthetic work, *Foundations of Christian Faith.* Chapters 1 to 3 are an analysis of the thinking believer (the discussions of "God" are preliminary and phenomenological). Those philosophical analyses (drawn from philosophies important during Rahner's lifetime but not selected by him as the only ways of reflecting on human life) are followed by chapter 4 where God's revelation and grace enter as an event in persons. The human and the divine come together in the remaining five chapters: in history leading to and from Jesus, in the teaching and person of Jesus, and in the history and fulfillment of the Christian message. In the midst of the human person God dwells, and the incarnation of Jesus is the visible statement of that invisible, constant reality.

> God's real supernatural and personal revelation is always being given. Hence the history of the human person and the history of revelation are coextensive. What we usually call revelation history (from Abraham and Moses to Jesus Christ) is not, strictly speaking, the history of revelation but a special and privileged part of that global salvation history constituted by God's self-communication as part of human existence and encountered throughout humanity's history at different levels.[38]

The following chapters unfold these three themes within person, religion, revelation, and church life.

III. REORIENTATIONS

"World of Grace," "Experience of Grace," "History of Grace"—commentators on Rahner use these phrases to title their books. God is present and experienced as more than the Creator, as God assisting, loving, and teaching human subjectivity.

> First and foremost, his theology of grace has most forcefully influenced modern theology through the universal will of God to save . . . , the extension of grace to those who would not seek baptism . . . , and the call of grace as a real and existential aspect of every person.[39]

The experience of God in men and women—this exists in a long history and in a global family. How do people from varied backgrounds, as they bow before a statue or read a sacred text, understand themselves and the divine? Does not God's love touch those who rarely think about God or religion? The social supports for the religious dimension (people more and more live in a secularized and pluralistic society) fall away, and yet beneath every historical shift there is a God seeking to be known in life and faith.[40]

> In an *ultimate* sense God is equally near everywhere. . . . The world is drawn to its spiritual fulfillment by the Spirit of God who directs the whole history of the world in all its length and breadth towards its proper goal. This means that every human person, whatever the situation, can be saved.[41]

Rahner moved away from a mechanics of graces entering into or withdrawing from the individual's will. Catholic spiritualities of grace had, from 1560 to 1960, depicted grace as a force, an extrinsic power suspended between the divine and the human. Divine forces moved a human faculty toward some religious end in adolescent decisions, receiving sacraments like marriage and orders, death-bed decisions, confessions, and spiritual direction. That psychology of celestial forces—often more human than divine—had a mechanistic tone as it arranged networks where generic divine forces came momentarily to sacraments, devotions, ideas, medals, and prayers.[42] Catholics developed, in the early modern centuries, a force field of devotions and rituals. Theologians in the mid-twentieth century pointed out the "extrinsicism" of this understanding of grace, for the divine presence stayed outside the person. Not only the passing force of grace, calculated sins, and church leadership, but even God was extrinsic to the modern person; many of Rahner's writings were indirectly or directly facing this immature theology.

> At one time, grace, assisting grace, and the outward circumstances shaped by God's grace in human life were conceived extrinsically, as discrete realities that occurred now and then, and which could be lacking

completely in the sinner or the unbeliever. My basic theological conviction opposes this. . . . For me grace is a reality which is so very much
part of the innermost core of human existence in decision and freedom,
always and above all given in the form of an offer that is either accepted
or rejected.[43]

Similarly, evil and sin were isolated actions, and their penetration into societies and persons was overlooked by endlessly evaluating bad actions.

Grace, however, is not the brief effect of a holy medal or a rapid
ritual but the presence of the Trinity in the graced person, a perduring,
silent dialogue with God. God does not come rarely to a small group,
nor does God withdraw when neglected, insulted, or opposed. Setting
aside the dualism oscillating between an impersonal human nature and
a transitory divine power, and moving beyond any fundamentalism
dividing the haves from the have-nots (Catholics from non-Catholics,
sacred clergy from profane laity), Rahner expressed anew the human
being surrounded by, offered, and implicitly seeking a presence of the
divine. John Galvin concludes:

> Rahner's treatment of diverse issues, ranging from the purpose of the
> sacraments to the question of salvation outside the church, are in large
> part a pursuit of the implications of his understanding of grace, helping
> to overcome false dichotomies and to transform Catholic thought in a
> number of respects. Contemporary discussions of the relationship of
> Christianity to other religions, of liberation theology, and of Christian
> spirituality are all cases in point.[44]

The wide extent of grace in a hundred thousand years before Abraham
and the billions of worshipers around the world does not diminish God
but affirms the divine wisdom, love, and power as it removes God from
being a feeble watcher of sinners or a largely failed restorer of human
goodness.

> It was Rahner's achievement to develop a new theology—one which
> safeguarded the free divine initiative and yet avoided seeing grace as
> a foreign element in the universe, extrinsic to the world in which we
> live. . . . God's self-gift to the world was not limited to the interior life
> of isolated individuals; in keeping with the social, historical dimension of
> human existence, grace freely offered necessarily sought public expres-
> sion in human history. In Jesus, God's self-gift reached its unsurpassable
> historical climax; so too did the history of its human acceptance.[45]

Not located solely in the soul or the tabernacle, in the next life or in the
pages of a religious books, grace is personal and social, radically divine
and active, Christian and universal. The Incarnation influences public

religion, economics, and politics, while the Body of the risen Christ draws ministries to lead church and society.

A new theology of grace after 1960 brought five "reorientations," five rediscoveries of the human, five turns toward the divine. The new orientations give a primacy to God's free plan for each person participating in God's life. *First,* the understanding of revelation and grace moves from verbal sentences and devotional routines to the divine presence as the origin and ground of all that pertains to faith and religion. *Second,* images for picturing the arrival of teaching and help from God move from a mechanics where human causality summons forth divine interventions to a personal God sharing its transcendent life and terrestrial plan. *Third,* God's teaching and assistance begin at deep levels of consciousness, in an unexpressed mode; later this presence (not at first verbalized) will employ human language and ritual. *Fourth,* Christianity is not primarily a biblical or ecclesiastical warehouse of stories and talismans but a presence that works through the history of cultures and people. *Finally,* theology moves away from the model of the single line dividing a small elite from the rest of human beings (Christians vs. Hindus, clergy vs. laity) to a model of concentric circles in which, with Christ as the center, grace is present and realized in varying degrees. Galvin offers a coda to this theme of the graced person.

To understand this theology of grace is to understand the totality of this theology. The many essays, whether treating of the Incarnation or the papacy, unfold from the reality of grace in human life. What is the essence of Christianity? "The only really absolute mysteries are the self-communication of God in the depths of existence, called grace, and in history, called Jesus Christ, and they already include the mystery of the Trinity."[46]

NOTES

1. *F* 2.

2. Albert Görres "Wer ist Karl Rahner für mich?—Antwort eines Psychotherapeuten," in Paul Imhof and Hubert Biallowons, eds., *Karl Rahner. Bilder eines Lebens* (Freiburg: Herder, 1985) 80.

3. "Introduction," Rahner, *Hearer of the Word* (New York: Continuum, 1994) xviii.

4. *FW* 10. "I never claimed to be a scientific researcher either in philosophy or in theology. I never practiced theology as a sort of art for art's sake. I think I can say that my publications usually grew out of pastoral concern" (Ibid., 174).

5. Metz, "Karl Rahners Ringen um die theologische Ehre des Menschen," *Stimmen der Zeit* 119 (1994) 383.

6. See "Reflections on Methodology in Theology," *TI* 11, 78–82.

7. Harold Schöndorf, "Vorwort," *Die philosophischen Quellen der Theologie Karl Rahners* (Freiburg: Herder, 2005) 7.

8. On Rahner's relationship to marginal believers and agnostics, see James J. Bacik, *Apologetics and the Eclipse of Mystery. Mystagogy according to Karl Rahner* (Notre Dame: University of Notre Dame Press, 1980) ch. 1.

9. "Karl Rahner," in W. Ernst Böhm, ed., *Forscher und Gelehrte* (Stuttgart: Battenberg, 1966) 21.

10. "The Future of Theology," *TI* 11, 141ff.

11. See Mathew Vekathanam, *Christology in the Indian Anthropological Context* (New York: P. Lang, 1986); Joseph Pandiappallil, *Jesus Christ and Religious Pluralism: Rahnerian Christology and Belief Today* (New York: Crossroad, 2001); on Latin America, see n. 22.

12. Karl Lehmann, "Karl Rahner zum Gedächtnis," *Stimmen der Zeit* 212 (1994) 148f. "New generations who have to overcome an initial shyness or reluctance about approaching him will find a great deal that is of value, will find help in recovering facets of Christianity that have faded away in our time or been deformed. Karl Rahner is someone for the day after tomorrow" (Ibid., 149). Linking Rahner to the theologies of Metz, Gustavo Gutiérrez, and David Tracy is Gaspar Martinez, "Catholic Post-Rahnerian Theology: Encountering the Mystery of God in History and Society" (Ph.D. dissertation, University of Chicago, 1997).

13. Lehmann selected as characteristics of Rahner's theology the pervasive influence of history, the rejection of a past positivism of religious data, faith seeking insight in the riches of the spirit, the centrality of the subject and grace, and a pastoral and practical tone ("Introduction," *The Content of the Faith* [New York: Crossroad, 1992] 1–42). Bernd Jochen Hilberath singles out efforts in a post-conciliar time at the end of the twentieth century to give a human orientation rather than a mechanical or scholastic apparatus and to stress the theme of the human person as the mystery of God, the self-communication of God, and Jesus as the bringer of salvation bestowed by a God willing the salvation of all (*GM* 24–45).

14. *KRD* 18; see the summary of this transcendental and existential anthropology grounding theology in Andrew Tallon, *Personal Becoming. In Honor of Karl Rahner at 75* (Milwaukee: Marquette University Press, 1982).

15. Donald Gelpi's writings treat Rahner and American philosophers of religion. "Why, then, does Rahner's theology enjoy such popularity among contemporary Catholics? . . . In a strange, paradoxical way, Rahner's turn to experience motivates his popularity. His turn to experience appeals for its plausibility to two fundamental human experiences . . . , the common human experience of mystery, and . . . implicitly to the adult conversion experience of cradle Christians" (*The Turn to Experience in Contemporary Theology* [New York: Paulist Press, 1994] 103f.); on Rahner's "personalist" theology and spirituality see Marek Chojnacki, *Die Nähe des Unbegreifbaren. Der moderne philosophische Kontext der Theologie Karl Rahners und seine Konsequenzen in dieser Theologie* (Fribourg: Universitätsverlag, 1996) 359ff., 135f.

16. "Church and World," *SM* 1, 347. "Hence the world or aeon 'to come' is already present and operative in the present world. It is clear from this that while

Christianity recognizes a certain dualism between God and world in redemptive history, a dualism which is already in process of dissolution, its does not acknowledge any radical and insuperable dualism. No such dualism should secretly color the practical life of Christians" (Ibid.).

17. *The Spirit in the Church* (New York: Seabury, 1979) 13.

18. *F* 40.

19. "On the Situation of the Catholic Intellectual," *TI* 8, 106–8.

20. L. Bruno Puntel, "Zu den Begriffen 'Transzendental' und 'Categorical' bei Karl Rahner," *WT* 197; see Andrew Tallon, "Introduction," Rahner, *Hearer of the Word* (New York: Continuum, 1994) x–xix.

21. *F* 61, 64. "Insofar as this subjective, non-objective luminosity of the subject in its transcendence is always orientated towards the holy mystery, the knowledge of God is always present unthematically and without name, and not just when we begin to speak of it" (*F* 21).

22. "Thoughts on the Theology of Christmas," *TI* 3, 25f. For a presentation of the transcendental anthropology of a theology of grace, see Francis Fiorenza, "Introduction," *Spirit in the World* (New York: Herder and Herder, 1968); Thomas Sheehan, *Karl Rahner. The Philosophical Foundations* (Athens, OH: Ohio University Press, 1987); Johannes Herzgsell, *Dynamik des Geistes. Ein Beitrag zum anthropologischen Transzendenzbegriff von Karl Rahner* (Innsbruck: Tyrolia, 2000). As J. B. Metz observed, the rather individualistic theology of Rahner needed to be given a political expansion (*Theology of the World* [New York: Seabury, 1969]); see Titus Guenther, *Rahner and Metz: Transcendental Theology as Political Theology* (Lanham, MD: University Press of America, 1994). Liberation theologians did apply Rahner to a practical world; see the essays by Juan Carlos Scannone and others in Karl Rahner, ed., *Befreiende Theologie. Der Beitrag Lateinamerikas zur Theologie der Gegenwart* (Stuttgart: Kohlhammer, 1977); Jon Sobrino, "Karl Rahner and Liberation Theology," *Theology Digest* 32 (1985) 257–60; Martin Maier, "Karl Rahner: Ignacio Ellacuría's Teacher," in Kevin F. Burke, s.j., and Robert Lassalle-Klein, eds., *Love that Produces Hope: The Thought of Ignacio Ellacuría* (Collegeville: Liturgical Press, 2005). Rahner, in his seventies, paid attention to liberation theology, and Jon Sobrino sees his influence on that theology to consist in an emphasis upon the primacy of reality, an existential format for faith, the reality of the mystery of God, theology as leading to mystery and as a spirituality, the sacramental character of reality, and the unity of the history of God in the world ("Gedanken über Karl Rahner aus Lateinamerika," *Stimmen der Zeit* 129 [2004] 43–56). Rahner edited a volume on liberation theology where his theology led not to a particular political direction or a Germanic or Brazilian political theology but to a theology of praxis in which political and economic directions were addressed and criticized. "In a letter to the Cardinal of Lima, Karl Rahner wrote two weeks before his death, 'The voice of the poor must be able to be heard.' That guarantees that Rahner understood the heart of liberation theology" (J. Sobrino, "Theologie der Befreiung," *KRB* 146); see Gerard O'Hanlon, "The Jesuits and Modern Theology—Rahner, von Balthasar and Liberation Theology," *The Irish Theological Quarterly* 58 (1992) 25–45.

23. *The Spirit in the Church,* 13.

24. *Everyday Faith* (New York: Herder and Herder, 1968) 110.

25. McCool, *The Theology of Karl Rahner* (Albany, NY: Magi Books, 1961) 41; "By no means do I claim transcendental anthropology as the only possibility. I see it only as a way to clarify something that is" (*FW* 21). There are similarities in format, if not in content, between Paul Tillich and Karl Rahner, and a fuller comparison (building upon a few dissertations in this area) remains to be done.

26. *F* 2.

27. *The Spirit in the Church*, 15.

28. *R* 410. "Wherever we find primarily the idea of an angry God who, as it were, has to be conciliated by great effort on the part of Jesus, we have an ultimately un-Christian, popular notion of redemption that is incorrect. This by no means denies that the holy God rejects sin absolute, and in that sense is 'angry' with the sinner. But this rejection always coexists in God with his desire to forgive and to overcome human sin" ("The Christian Understanding of Redemption," *TI* 21, 249).

29. *The Eternal Year* (Baltimore: Helicon, 1964) 66–72.

30. *R* 410f.

31. *F* 119. Rahner became known for bringing together different aspects of the theology of the Trinity, observing that the Trinity as revealed by Jesus as active in salvation history is the source for what we know about the Trinity immanent in the divine being; see *The Trinity* (New York: Crossroad, 1997).

32. *The Spirit in the Church*, 9–13. A few English-speaking critics have overlooked that there are two words in German for "experience": "*Erlebnis*" and "*Erfahrung.*" The first is emotional experience; the second, without an English counterpart, is contact with a reality in a deep, general, not always expressed ("transcendental") mode; see "Religious Enthusiasm and the Experience of Grace," *TI* 16, 35–51.

33. Mühlen, "Gnadenlehre," *Bilanz der Theologie* 3 (Freiburg: Herder, 1970) 161.

34. Anne Carr, "Karl Rahner," in Dean G. Peerman and Martin Marty, eds., *A Handbook of Christian Theologians: Enlarged Edition* (Nashville: Abingdon, 1984) 524.

35. "Historicity and transcendentality are the most difficult to understand of all the fundamental structures of human existence" (*KRD* 132); see Bernd Jochen Hilberath, "Jesus Christus. Der absolute Heilbringer," *GM* 118–45.

36. "THEOS in the New Testament," *TI* 1, 86.

37. *F* 141.

38. Rahner, "*Reflections on* Foundations of the Christian Faith," *Theology Digest* 28 (1980) 209, 211.

39. Karl-Heinz Weger, "Zur Theologie Karl Rahners," *GB* 88. Roman Siebenrock calls this theology of grace "the principle giving form to all of [his] theology" (Siebenrock, "Gnade als Herz der Welt. Der Beitrag Karl Rahners zu einer zeitgemässen Gnadentheologie," *TEG* 34–41).

40. *KRD*, 21f., 23f.

41. "The One Christ and the Universality of Salvation," *TI* 16, 204.

42. See Stephen Duffy, *The Graced Horizon* (Collegeville: Liturgical Press, 1992).

43. *FW* 21.

44. John Galvin, "Grace for a New Generation," *Commonweal* 112 (1985) 42; *F* 398–401. Already in one of his first articles, published in 1939, Rahner had found a

new direction for the theology of grace, going beyond the transitory force to a vital form of human life, a forgotten aspect of Aquinas's theology ("Some Implications of the Scholastic Concept of Uncreated Grace," *TI* 1, 319–46); on Rahner's courses on grace in the years from 1930 to 1960, see *DKR* 111–25.

45. Galvin, "Grace for a New Generation," 42.

46. *F* 12.

Chapter 4

Men and Women within God's Life

Karl Rahner was a traditional revolutionary. New ways of thinking in the twentieth century drew out personal and ecclesial elaborations of what he held to be the fundamental reality of Christianity: God's loving plan present in each person. Rahner was no academic critic of religion, dismissing every entry of God in human life (theologies of reduction, of demythologization had, as was obvious by 1970, driven believers away). Rather, he described anew God's life incarnate in movements and people. The sacramental was the real.

While the reality of God's special presence (what Jesus called the reign of God and theologians since Paul have named grace) has for its teacher, center, and cause Jesus Christ, it enters all of history with billions of people. Consequently, his gift of holy life to human beings must have several modalities of contacting people, of drawing the human person forward to a special word and life coming from God.

I. THE SEEKING PERSON, THE REVEALING GOD

Through a lifetime, a person searches for meaning, hope, and fulfillment, and, too, the love of God encounters each man and woman in all aspects of life, not just in religion.

> The secular world, as secular, has an inner mysterious depth, in all its earthly mysteries from birth to death through which, by the grace of God, it is open to God and his infinitely incomprehensive love even when it is not before receiving the explicit message of the Gospel aware of it. Not

only are there many anonymous Christians; there is also an anonymous Christian world. For whenever its demands and its reality are really met and endured in the whole breadth and depth of human existence and in the totality of human life . . . the grace of Christ is already at work.[1]

What does the Christian faith say to the contemporary person aware of life as a journey? Is the Gospel more than unfounded rules or devotions bordering on the superstitious? Are there people who no longer have any ear for the word of God in its deepest meaning for their existence? Are there ever people who no longer inquire beyond the endless variety of questions into "the more?"

> Decisive situations in the course of a human life might appear at first to appear as profane, but they too are situations of a saving history. They compel the individual to look freely at the totality, and at the particularity of his or her own life, to face the mystery and the absurdity, to have a glimpse of the inconceivable love that stands near to him.[2]

The Jesuit was always learning about people. He did not equate psychology with faith or grace. Human self-transcendence searching for fulfillment leads to God even as it already holds subtly the divine.

> God is not just the partner who stands opposite a human being in such a way that as a result of an odd synergism and reciprocal influence something or other happens that goes by the name of human redemption. God is, rather, the one who creates human beings as well as their freedom. . . . And it is this God who by his free and absolute act of grace makes it possible for human beings to redeem themselves, so to speak.[3]

God addresses the human person in her freedom, history, and existential life.

The great religious question is not about the existence of a deity but about God's attitude toward us. The existence of God (largely the occupation of logicians) is not the message of Christian revelation but its presupposition. To conclude through a proof drawn from logic or physics that there is a supreme being

> leaves God, however, unknown, since God becomes something known to us only through analogy, and as mystery, becomes known through mediate intellection which occurs only through a negative passing beyond the finite and not directly by laying hold of God. . . . Thus it remains unknown whether God intends (or is able) to be for us the absolute intimacy of radical self-communication, or a silent, self-contained infinity keeping us imprisoned at a distance in our finitude; or further, whether God's response to our sinful rejection of God would be judgment or forgiveness.[4]

Christianity opens an entry into mystery, "mystagogy," empowering a journey toward and in the self-communication of God. Beyond feelings and rituals, philosophy and aesthetics, there is a true revelation of God. God is much more than the source of the universe.

> God's supernatural offering of himself to the created spirit is the in-nermost and ultimate characteristics of the human person in its total reality (and not something added to whatever else human nature has). Creation, as it in fact exists, is an element in the fundamental miracle of divine love in which God wills to give himself. Despite its supernatural character, therefore the order of grace is not in respect of the world a supplementary orientation added afterwards, directing towards higher but extrinsic goals. It is the world's innermost characteristic from the outset, not because it is demanded by the world's constitution but as self-transcendence, above and beyond what it is, towards immediate re-lationship with God. . . . Everything proceeds from this saving will of God and is objectively directed towards the goal of that will, everything according to its mode of being.[5]

Christianity proclaims a universal plan and will by God for each and all. At some level of consciousness God speaks to all men and women without drawing the divine down into this world, without becoming an idol, and without making his message ridiculous or impossible to understand.

> A supernatural goal for humanity, freely established by God, is always implanted in the being of every person through the self-communication of God in grace on account of the universal saving will of God in advance of every free decision, and so it exists in each person either in the mode of acceptance or refusal.[6]

An "anonymous" or "implicit" or "general" belief in God means that, from the Christian point of view, something of the reality revealed by Jesus (but not the person or his words) is glimpsed and accepted when love and faith and hope are present in life. Rahner sought light in a prayer:

> I would like a final answer to the deepest mystery that I am to myself. I would like to have something to do with God. I would like to have an ulti-mate hope for the validity and true reality of my existence. I wouldn't like to be consumed by the banality of the everyday. I would like to see myself in solidarity with the people of the past who are not simply the precondi-tion of some kind of utopian future of success and consumerism.

And he concluded with a question: "Where can we find an answer to these and hundreds of other similar questions outside of Christianity?

For Christianity's unique message endures precisely in its answer to each of the questions just raised: there is a final hope."[7]

II. HUMAN EXISTENCE IN GOD'S REALM

Each man and woman is ordinary and special; God is distant and yet easily accessible.

What people call redemption and salvation is not a distant religious or judicial process by which a miserable sinner escapes divine condemnation, but God's gift of self to a person created for love and life. The incarnation in Jesus affirms that there can be an intimate relationship in life between the absolute and the dependent.

What religions name "revelation" and "grace" comes first in a deep presence of God that contacts people in various ways.

> In this unnamed and uncharted expanse of our consciousness there dwells that which we call God, not a special, particularly unusual piece of objective reality, something to be added to and included in the other realities of our naming and classifying experience but the comprehensive though never comprehended ground and presupposition of our experience and of the objects of that experience.[8]

The acceptance of life and of self, the service of others, is the gift of a silent Mystery seeking to fill the emptiness of people.

> Wherever people live selfless lives, whenever they truly make the leap into mystery, into unearned love, into a final and radical truth, they are dealing with God and have received God's Spirit. The question whether they can define it as such or verbalize it may be important humanly speaking—for faith or theology—but in the end it is of secondary importance.[9]

God's self-sharing is in Rahner's phrase a "supernatural existential." The word "existential" (borrowed from Heidegger) indicates an aspect of human life, a reality of existence. A supernatural existential is a form not phenomenologically seen but held by faith to be real and present, "present in every person at least in the mode of an offer."[10] To exist on earth is to exist within the reign of God as a real possibility and potentiality. "Really and radically every person must be understood as the event of the supernatural self-communication of God, although not in the sense that every person necessarily accepts in freedom God's self-communication to man."[11] The offer and beginning of grace are not a justifying badge or a mechanical network of helps coming to a neutral person. The supernatural existential is not an object but an invisible yet real constitution of a person by God: it is "supernatural" because it belongs to a realm fashioned by God beyond the cosmos of minerals and life-forms; it is "existential" because a constant offer of divine love touches not the nature of Greek philosophy, but the full human existence of modernity. "In every human being there is something like an anonymous, unthematic, perhaps repressed basic experience of being orientated to God (which is constitutive of man in his concrete make-up of nature and grace) and which can be repressed but not destroyed."[12]

This offer of grace brings "objective" justification but not necessarily "subjective" salvation. Each person can receive and enact grace.

> Whenever a person in full and free self-disposition performs a moral act, in the actual order of salvation that act is also a positive supernatural salvific act. This is so even if its *a posteriori* object and express motives do not obviously stem from the revealed word of God but are in this sense "natural." For, by his general salvific will, God offers divinizing grace to each man and elevates supernaturally his positive moral acts.[13]

A realization of this existential mode comes from a further act, a free acceptance of God by the individual.

> People can achieve the ultimate purpose of their existence outside the church. The church explicitly teaches that you can find salvation without the church as an intermediary by following your conscience. That does not mean that you can win heaven with just good will and without that which is essential to Christian existence. . . . People who do not know anything about Christ are not saved because the "poor devils" couldn't help it. Rather, it presumes that they know God in a way that includes a genuine faith and a corresponding hope and love . . . , the wonder which God's grace awakens in the innermost center of our concrete lives.[14]

Each man and woman lives in a world, which, according to Christian faith, is a world of grace.

> There is one who is silent although he could defend himself, although he is unjustly treated, who keeps silence without feeling that his silence is his sovereign unimpeachability.

> There is a man who obeys not because he must and would otherwise find it inconvenient to disobey, but purely on account of that mysterious, silent and inconceivable thing that we call God and the will of God.

> There is a man who renounces something without thanks or recognition, and even without a feeling of inner satisfaction. There is a man who is absolutely lonely, who finds all the right elements of life pale shadows; for whom all trustworthy handholds take him into the infinite distance,

and who does not run away from this loneliness but treats it with ultimate hope.

> There is one who suddenly notices how the tiny trickle of his life wanders through the wilderness of the banality of existence, apparently without aim and with the heartfelt fear of complete exhaustion without knowing that this trickle will find the infinite expanse of the ocean, even though it may still be covered by the grey sands, which seem to extend forever before him.[15]

Rahner was a theological psychologist of the human life. The supernatural existential calls through personality and society to God's life. Clearly, even for the person baptized, life presents decades of responding to offers of grace, of letting a facet of existence become an existential relationship to Jesus, personal and individual.

Grace and revelation go beyond the constant silent offer to the explicit level, incarnation, reaching the reality of Jesus Christ, now and in the eschaton. Revelation, the message of God's love and future, comes to a climax in God's Word, Jesus. The teaching of Jesus itself emerges from the silent conversation of the Spirit dwelling within. "This address is a part of the whole process of revelation and not simply a phase anterior in time or an isolated event."[16] What this means is that the history of salvation recorded in the Bible is not a series of accidents and misfortunes, but a history that in its parts and in its totality recounts how grace and revelation survive evil and sin. A shift of grace from the rituals of temples to the depth of people is, as we have stressed, not a move toward secularity or the absence of liturgy. The shared life of God does not disdain but embraces time and culture and lets emerge a myriad of sacramental circles and points of power that Catholics find in a world of grace. This incarnational dynamic is the atmosphere of Earth.

III. AN ORDINARY SPIRITUALITY

People who begin with Karl Rahner's philosophical writings or with academic articles on transcendental knowing are surprised that Rahner composed prayers and wrote essays on the spiritual life. Setting aside divisions between theory and praxis, he saw the daily life of believers and the ministries of the church as animated by the Holy Spirit, friend, mentor, and guide. For the son of Ignatius Loyola, spirituality is not a private mysticism nor a psychological exercise but an existential and transcendental praxis discerning the triune God in daily life.

Spirituality is theology made personal. An individual selects aspects of Christian teaching. In spirituality a dogmatics is personalized, a theology made concrete; the psychological and personal focus the message of Christianity into personal application, into charismatic founder, into lasting school. An explanation of faith beginning with the transcendental modality of divine grace contacting the mystery of human freedom and a theology employing words like "decision," "orientation," "unfolding," and "realization" is a spirituality.

> Christianity ultimately (I say "ultimately," not "alone") announces that the absolute, infinite, holy, and living God is the total fulfillment of human existence. Then with that comes a joy and a fulfillment of a fundamental kind exceeding everything else. Whether, and how far, an individual man or woman in the concrete situations of life, limited by one's lifespan, by one's work, depending also upon one's individual, intellectual and other abilities, is able to really appreciate such an awesome message is quite another question. Nevertheless, Christianity preaches an absolute joy.[17]

Karl Lehmann and Albert Raffelt assembled a "book of spiritual reading," a collection of texts by Rahner about themes in spirituality and pastoral theology like vocation and perseverance. The inspirational is simultaneously theological. "Karl Rahner is not only an architect of modern Catholic theology but at the same time a master in the exercise of the Christian life."[18] Here spirituality and theology are facets of the same reality, of existential grace, individual faith, ordinary mysticism. Herbert Vorgrimler comments:

> This mysticism is (as a spirituality) not at all eccentric or withdrawn; it does not produce a balanced condition of the soul bothered by nothing; it is not like the techniques and promises of certain gurus. Similarly the basic and accompanying theology is not the solution to all puzzles and questions, a system that resolves every issue whose data can prove a dogma or produce a psychological passivity. Rahner's mysticism—it is not one of the middle of the road, of serene balance or of irrational trust—pursues a course always incomplete in the practice of concrete love.[19]

Fellow Jesuits note how this spirituality flows from an Ignatian inspiration and consequently is attentive to the concrete, the real, and the active. In a life of faith there is the course of daily life with its struggles vitalized by a deeper consciousness of God not as an object but as a person. A subliminal dialogue between mystery and psychology holds immediacy to God's love that surpasses all ideas and object. This spirituality begins with the silence of divine presence and the activities of the human personality and ends in the courageous advocacy of the renewal of society and the church. Rahner wrote on Jesuit spirituality. He pondered devotion to the Sacred Heart of Jesus and penned prayers; he often gave the *Spiritual Exercises* and he published a book of his reflections on them. There he gives the major Ignatian themes a markedly Germanic interpretation, drawing Christian life into the dialectic of Being and beings. This and other great writings of mysticism are important because they are a "creative prototype . . . [and] a subject of tomorrow's theology."[20] Suffice it to say that Ignatius is a Christian living at the beginning of the modern era (like Luther), and his spirituality unfolds a theology that is also a psychology, an analysis of the active self in service of the kingdom. One can move, as Belgian, French, and German Jesuits of the first half of this century showed, from Ignatian spirituality to the thought-forms of modernity. The Ignatian theology of active grace finds the spiritual in all things; the search is transcendental and categorical.

Much is made of Rahner's line that increasingly believers will be mystics. It is not helpful, however, to confuse his central theme of grace and revelation surrounding each human subject in a silent but dynamic way with what is meant since the sixteenth century by mysticism, or to see his theology mainly as a modern spirituality. Protestants have mistakenly thought that his references to the experience of grace had something to do with the emotional. The self heightened by an ordinary though supernatural presence of God finds herself in the surrounding world, and grace leads out into church and society. The acting person is the place of God's personal presence, much more than a subject arranging methods and prayers. Rahner's theology looks at every aspect of the human personality and ends not in emotion or introspection but in thinking and acting.[21] This is not exactly what the world "mystic" means. Declan Marmion finds in Rahner's spirituality a Christocentric focus and also dimensions of ministry and liturgy. Further, drawing on Jon Sobrino and Anne Carr, he sees links with liberation theology and feminism.[22]

Fashioned from a spirituality for contemporary life, one of his prayers to the Holy Spirit ends:

> If it is your will to lead us on such difficult paths, then we implore you, send us at least during these days and hours the Holy Spirit of faithfulness, steadfastness, and perseverance, so that we can go forward with blind confidence, holding to our route and remaining true to the resolutions which we choose when your light showed us the path and your joy enlarged our heart. Give us always a spirit of bravery and of bold resolve, to recognize temptation, not to dispute with it nor to compromise, but to give it an unequivocal refusal, for this is the simplest strategy. Give us the spirit of wisdom to see the real danger points of our characters and lives, to keep watch and to contend most constantly where we are most

vulnerable. Jesus send us the Spirit. Give us again and again your Pentecostal gift.[23]

Spirituality presents a theology, prepares for a ministry, welcomes the Spirit into an ordinary Christian life.

IV. DRAMAS OF GRACE

The human drama becomes tangible and visible in the arts. For the believer, art makes divine grace human. Faith and art, ecstasy and inspiration aspire to the transcendent and the transcendental, while insight and faith have similarities with art and liturgy. Exploring human psychological depth and divine presence, theology (like art) speaks not only in abstract concepts about theological questions but must also introduce people to an experience of the reality it proclaims. Rahner's few essays on art stress human experience as the source of art, and so, like theology, arts open into the depths of grace. The more art draws the person into the drama of sin and grace, the more it is like a theology challenging faith.[24] The arts in their modern styles depict the presence of God in ways that do not always use explicitly religious stories and figures. Religious images remind the viewer of what she already knows and believes. Art's religious message is not limited by religious figures like those in Raphael's paintings or Bach's cantatas. Is any experience of depth exclusively secular? Art is not a flight from history and individual life, but their expression. The artist is a discoverer of visible and audible ways to express transcendental and graced life in a new and original way.[25] "If theology is the conscious self-expression of persons about themselves from the point of view of divine revelation, we might submit the view that the most perfect kind of theology would be one appropriating the arts as an integral part of themselves."[26]

Rahner's theology helps in understanding the religious dynamic shaping some literature of the modern period. From World War II through the 1960s, as Catholic theologians in Europe were fashioning subtle and complex theologies, replacing the easy mechanics of divine causes and effects inherited from the Baroque, Catholic novelists wrote of the complexity of the modern person. In the twentieth century, Catholicism was moving from the abstract to the personal. In fact, the heart of the Catholic worldview is not obedience to papal authority, new Marian apparitions, or a church service attended briefly each Sunday, but incarnation. Without a theology of the subtleties of grace and sin, it is not easy to understand the fiction of François Mauriac, Georges Bernanos, and Flannery O'Connor (or the paintings of Kandinsky or

Rothko). In the twentieth century there was a religious fiction, often written by Catholic novelists, that looks not at rosaries and cloisters but at agnostics and adulterers, at martyrs and revolutionaries, because the poignant drama of a life displays sin and grace emotionally.

In some of Graham Greene's novels, the religious world, their Catholicism, pursues the theme of grace touching human lives amid hope and misery. Salvation comes not through rituals and words but through a silent divine word within human faith. The things of religion at best manifest grace, serve the divine presence in momentary concrete forms, while mercy and love are more important. The forms of religion can fail, can obscure or pervert spiritual life, and the inner depth of grace can be present in someone who for mature and spiritual reasons rejects church and dogma. Human life can be moral without being explicitly Christian, loving without being ecclesiastical.[27] Rahner's theology of the universal presence of the hidden God and of the graced openness of daily life invited Christians to see other people differently.[28]

Rahner alluded to the British novelist:

> If I read . . . a novel by someone like Graham Greene, which, to be sure, cannot simply "contain" an immediate and genuine religious experience, for that is quite impossible, but which perhaps evokes in me my own experience of the religious, then this literature has accomplished something which reflexive, purely conceptual and rational theology is not able to accomplish.[29]

Rahner's theology of grace shows some resemblance to the religious ethos in Greene's fiction, although such similarities do not imply a dependency or mutual knowledge between novelist and theologian. Both rejected superficial ecclesiastical and verbal formats to describe a quest for identity. For Christianity should not be presenting a logician of theodicy, a distant deity of Calvinism, or a judge of nineteenth-century devotions, but a God helping a human person. While grace becomes explicit in creeds, rituals, and institutions, those concrete realizations are secondary and should be critiqued and renewed.

> If God's self-communication is an ultimate and radical modification of our personality in our daily dealings with any and every individual reality . . . , then this means in principle that the original experience of God, even in his self-communication, is so universal, so unthematic and so "unreligious" that it takes place—unnamed but really—wherever we are living out our existence.[30]

Religious doctrines sometimes help Greene's characters to interpret life, although they can also hold faith captive in a destructive belief or piety. His depictions of religious weakness do not imply a rejection of all forms of belief. In life as in fiction both invisible lust or love and visible sacrament and help are the human forms of grace or sin. "It is the person," Rahner wrote, "who in the forlornness of guilt still turns in trust to the mystery of existence quietly present, and then surrenders the self as one who even in guilt no longer wants to be self-centered and self-sufficient—this person experiences being forgiven."[31] Sin does not exclude the possibility of grace; suffering does not preclude transformation. "A person who opens the self to his or her transcendental experience of the ultimate holy mystery has the experience that this mystery is not simply an infinitely distant horizon, a remote judgment . . . but is also a hidden closeness, a forgiving intimacy, a real home."[32]

Greene's *A Burnt-Out Case* describes individuals searching for a realm wider and healthier than a clinic or a church, a power drawing men and women to their needed salvation. People do not talk religiously but they do talk about religion. In the equatorial rain forest of the Congo, Deo Gratias is a syncretist on a path of eschatological faith; Rycker's theological reading distracts him from curbing his violent personality; Fr. Thomas's asceticism and dogmatic clichés imprison him. Dr. Colin is an atheist and yet a man of love and service with a faith sustained by evolution and medicine rather than by sacraments. Greene purposely kept the forms of Catholicism or the denials of agnosticism on the surface as his characters struggle for their orientation. He spoke of the novelist being somewhat God-like in that he looked into the mystery of free will and predestination to grace. The characters' journeys into health, psychological and spiritual, depend upon a recognition and rediscovery of some goodness in people. Rahner concluded:

> The freedom to accept or refuse salvation occurs in all the dimensions of human existence, and it occurs always in an encounter with the world and not merely in the confined sector of the sacred or of worship and "religion" in the narrow sense. It occurs in encounters with one's neighbor, with one's historical task, with the so-called world of everyday life, in and with what we call the history of the individual and of communities.[33]

Faith and grace are not "primarily and ultimately the experience which a person has when he decides explicitly and in a deliberate and responsible way upon some *religious* activity, for example, prayer, a liturgical action, or a reflexive and theoretical occupation with religious theme."[34]

Doubt before dogma, actions beyond or against religious laws, superstitious religion—these are aspects of "a love which shares itself, something familiar which the person can approach and turn to, away

from the estrangement of his own perilous and empty life."[35] Imposing
a Christian dogma is not more religious than the love of a leper, and
human intention exists prior to and within external actions. Grace is
always at work leading people beyond "the bag of tricks" alienating
atheists or intriguing potential converts. The father-superior of the
priests, though naive about society's forms, has mature insights into the
continuing dialogue between human beings and God's grace, and like
Dr. Colin, his secular counterpart, he has outgrown the need to divide
the world into the baptized and the natives, the saints and the sinners.
His sermon to the congregation on who is a "Klistian" recalls Jesus'
preaching of a love of God open to all—and it recalls Rahner's theology of widespread grace. "Yezu made love, he made mercy. Everybody
in the world has something that Yezu made. Everybody in the world is
that much a Klistian. There is no man so wicked he never once in his
life show in his heart something that God made."[36] Rahner's theology of
divine self-sharing illumines Graham Greene's novels in two important
ways: grace is a real but secretly pervasive divine reality touching, heal-
ing, and leading free persons to actions of faith and love; the objects of
religious practice and teaching can aid or block, realize or obscure grace
in the orientation of each man or woman.

Individual life fashions drama: each of our lives will be a unique
drama of the struggle to respond to grace.

> The unity of a love that despises nothing and shuts out nothing, the unity
> of a love that endures smallness and remains open to greatness, a love
> that sees the world as a great parable, not a parable that is separate and
> apart, but a parable that is drawn into the great reality it represents. Our
> daily round of work is full of holy significance, a preparation for great-
> ness. And it is in the midst of this daily round that what is holy happens.
> The person of faith, of a serene insight into the events of his or her life is
> able to recognize the parable of each individual life.[37]

The events of our lives, small and great, have meaning and a unity. The
German novelist Heinrich Böll wrote:

> Modernity, the "todayness" of his hearers—he found that perhaps more
> in contemporary literature and art than in his own discipline. Karl Rah-
> ner was in an unusual way both open and closed, a risky combination,
> but the only possible one. It must have bothered him that his church had
> alienated itself so far from art and literature. . . . What was astonishing
> in Rahner was the believability of his own faith; high intelligence, high
> intellectual level but also sober and detached. He was a witness: a witness
> who not only gave witness but bore his own witness.[38]

The dynamic of grace bears daily life forward, enabling grace to flourish in colorful diversity. There is a world of grace, and there is a history of grace. It is that expanse of time the next chapter considers.

NOTES

1. "The Parish Bookshop," *Christian in the Market Place* (New York: Sheed and Ward, 1966) 97; on similarities between Rahner and Newman see Heinrich Fries, "Theological Method according to John Henry Newman and Karl Rahner," *Philosophy & Theology* 18 (2005) 43–59.

2. *Über die Sakramente der Kirche. Meditationen* (Freiburg: Herder, 1985 [1991]) 15. Pastoral theology should look at the course of grace and the psychology of development in nonpracticing Christians and, too, at the effectiveness of the church's pastoral outreach ("On the Structure of the People of God Today," *TI* 12, 224–6).

3. "The Christian Understanding of Redemption," *TI* 21, 240f.

4. *R* 410.

5. "Order," *SM* 4, 297f.

6. "Order," 301. The phrase "anonymous Christian" seems to have appeared first in 1962 in "Thoughts on the Possibility of Belief Today" (*TI* 5, 9–22). It meant not that members of other religions are Christians, but that they seek, receive, and are vivified by what Christian faith holds to be the ultimate divine presence ("the reign of God"). Rahner easily set the phrase aside, always pointing out that its meaning—implicit faith, wider grace—was part of Catholic tradition on salvation outside of baptism and explicit faith (Rahner "Anonymous Christianity," in Eugene Hillman, *The Wider Ecumenism* [London: Burns & Oates, 1968] 38). Already in 1947 he had written how "a member in the people of God has a quasi-sacramental structure. Because the human being is a concrete, corporeal human being, the blood relative of Christ, the *votum ecclesiae* does not happen in a purely extra-sacramental, purely invisible gracious interiority but is an act of a concrete human being essentially and necessarily taking on the quasi-sacramental structure which appropriates itself on the basis of the Incarnation of God to humanity" ("Membership of the Church according to Pius XII's Encyclical, 'Mystici Corpori Christi,'" *TI* 2, 1–88). For an extensive treatment of the phrase and the reality, see *SGW* and Schwerdtfeger, "Der anonyme Christ' in der Theologie Karl Rahner," *TEG* 70; recent writings on the theology of wider grace include David Coffey, "The Whole Rahner on the Supernatural Existential," *Theological Studies* 65 (2004) 104–18; Robert A. Burns, *Roman Catholicism after Vatican II* (Washington, D.C.: Georgetown University Press, 2000); Elmar Klinger, ed., *Christentum innerhalb und ausserhalb der Kirche* (Freiburg: Herder, 1976).

7. *KRD* 146f.

8. *The Spirit in the Church* (New York: Seabury, 1979) 14.

9. *KRD* 142. "God meets the human person basically in an anonymous way, always more present and present in a different way than what men and women easily experience, conceive or expect. God is the God of the mystery of human longings and hopes, discoveries and difficulties, of the entirety of the daily world. God is

silence in the agitation of hours without peace, the light in the darkness of unclear intentions, the guarantee of life in the network of unfulfilled desires" (Elmar Klinger, *Das absolute Geheimnis im Alltag entdecken. Zur spirituellen Theologie Karl Rahners* [Würzburg: Echter, 1994] 39).

10. *F* 127. Is not what is called original sin also an existential? It is not sin—no one after the proto-parents commits it—and not something done by anyone and yet it appears with each of us. It is a fallenness, an influential background of selfishness, an absence of grace or virtuous balance. Humans do not fashion it but receive it. "We are people who must inevitably exercise our own freedom subjectively in a situation which is co-determined by objectifications of guilt, and indeed in such a way that this co-determination belongs to our situation permanently and inescapable" (*F* 110).

11. *F* 128.

12. "Teresa of Avila: Doctor of the Church," *Opportunities for Faith* (New York: Seabury, 1970) 125.

13. "The Unity of God and Love of Neighbor," "Reflections on the Unity . . . ," *TI* 6, 243. "The duality we have just described is what Christians call sanctifying and justifying grace: a divinizing elevation of people ('created' grace) whereby God gives not only something different from himself ('habitual' grace) but his own self ('uncreated' grace) and empowers an individual to accept it ('actual' grace)" (*R* 410f.).

14. *KRD* 103.

15. *The Spirit in the Church* (New York: Seabury, 1979) 19–21; see *F* 306.

16. *R* 410.

17. *FW* 10.

18. Karl Lehmann, Albert Raffelt, eds., Karl Rahner. *Praxis des Glaubens. Geistliches Lesebuch* (Freiburg: Herder, 1982) 9.

19. Vorgrimler, "Gotteserfahrung im Alltag. Der Beitrag Karl Rahners zu Spiritualität und Mystik," *LGG* 77f.

20. *The Dynamic Element in the Church*, 86; see Rahner, *Spiritual Exercises* (London: Sheed and Ward, 1967). M. Schneider, *Unterscheidung der Geister. Die Ignatianischen Exerzitien in der Deutung von E. Przywara, K. Rahner and G. Fessard* (Innsbruck: Tyrolia, 1983); Thomas O'Meara, *Erich Przywara, s.j. His Theology and His World* (Notre Dame: University of Notre Dame Press, 2002) 150–5; Annice Callahan, *Karl Rahner's Spirituality of the Pierced Heart* (Lanham, MD: University Press of America, 1985); Andrew Tallon, "The Heart in Rahner's Philosophy of Mysticism," *TS* 53 (1992) 700–28; Elmar Klinger, *Das absolute Geheimnis im Alltag entdecken*, 47–54. The writings of Harvey Egan are helpful: *The Spiritual Exercises and the Ignatian Mystical Horizon* (St. Louis: Institute of Jesuit Sources, 1976); "The Devout Christian of the Future Will . . . Be a 'Mystic.'" Mysticism and Karl Rahner's Theology," in William J. Kelly, ed., *Theology and Discovery: Essays in Honor of Karl Rahner, s.j.* (Milwaukee: Marquette University Press, 1980) 139–68; *Karl Rahner. Mystic of Everyday Life* (New York: Crossroad, 1998); *What Are They Saying about Mysticism* (New York: Paulist, 1982); Philip Endean, *Karl Rahner and Ignatian Spirituality* (Oxford: Oxford University Press, 2004).

21. "Theologische Tugenden (Systematische)," *Lexikon für Theologie und Kirche* 10 (Freiburg: Herder, 1965) 80; "Works," *SM* 5, 373–5; on Rahner and ethics see

James F. Bresnahan, "An Ethics of Faith," *A World of Grace* (Washington, D.C.: Georgetown University Press, 1980) 169–84; "Rahner's Christian Ethics," *America* 123 (October 31, 1970); Ronald Modras, "Implications of Rahner's Anthropology for Fundamental Moral Theology," *Horizons* 12 (1985) 70–90; Timothy E. O'Connell, "The Question of Grundentscheidung," and David Coffey, "Rahner's Theology of Fundamental Option," in *Philosophy & Theology* 10 (1998) 143–68; 169–78; Engelbert Guggenberger, *Karl Rahners Christologie und heutige Fundamentalmoral* (Innsbruck: Tryolia, 1990).

22. Declan Marmion, *A Spirituality of Everyday Faith. A Theological Investigation of the Notion of Spirituality in Karl Rahner* (Louvain: Peeters, 1998) 312–36; 336–57; see Mary Hines, "Rahnerian Spirituality: Implications for Ministry," *Handbook of Spirituality for Ministers* (New York: Paulist, 1995) 129–40; Ralf Stolina, *Die Theologie Karl Rahners: Inkarnatorische Spiritualität. Menschwerdung Gottes und Gebet* (Innsbruck: Tyrolia, 1996).

23. *Prayers for a Lifetime* (New York: Commonweal, 1987) 87.

24. "Art against the Horizon of Theology and Piety," *TI* 23, 163.

25. "The Theology of the Religious Meaning of Images," *TI* 23, 159; see "Christ and Literature," *TI* 6, 8–19.

26. "Art against the Horizon of Theology and Piety," *TI* 23, 163.

27. *F* 116.

28. Elmar Klinger, *Das absolute Geheimnis im Alltag entdecken*, 36.

29. "Theology and the Arts," *Thought* 57 (1982) 25.

30. *F* 132.

31. *F* 131.

32. Ibid. "There is no positive and active predestination to sin, that is, to a misuse of freedom. Such a reality is inconceivable before the holiness of God and before his general will for salvation; speculatively it is not necessary since the sinfulness of the sinful act as a lack of being demands no positive divine causality. God does not will the sin even if he 'sees it in advance.' . . . The mystery of the relationship between the all-efficacious activity of God (with which predestination is given) and the proper freedom of the creature is simply the application at the level of activity of the mystery of a finite being which reality is, that is, which is different from God and which before him has its own valid causality and yet which precisely is ceaselessly born by God" ("Prädestination. Systematisch," *Lexikon für Theologie und Kirche* 8 [Freiburg: Herder, 1961] 669).

33. "History of the World and Salvation-History," *TI* 5, 98f.

34. *F* 131.

35. Ibid.

36. *A Burnt-Out Case* (New York: Viking, 1961) 98.

37. "Love Sees the World as a Parable," *Biblical Homilies* (New York: Herder and Herder, 1965) 39.

38. Heinrich Böll, "Auf der Suche nach einer neuen Sprache," in Paul Imhof and Hubert Biallowons, eds., *KRB* (Freiburg: Herder, 1985) 98.

Chapter 5

God's Life in Terrestrial History

People living in a city or at the edge of a desert, men and women in their cultural worlds of language and clothes and entertainment—each is seeking something more of life. Every religion reveals and serves the meeting of two persons: one Infinite, and one fragile and limited. A loving God fashions and touches the billions of searching individuals on planet Earth through forms of faith, hope, and love.

History liberates human quests for the divine. The history of a person or a culture becomes tangible in the words and rituals of a religion. The Jewish and Christian faiths with their Scriptures present a God acting in history, and, too, at the beginning, center, and destiny of the church is history. Some churches or religions ignore history, seeking a timeless meditation or a transcendent deity; or, they think only a small movement founded recently has the truth. Catholic theology before Vatican II was thoroughly ahistorical, arguing that all human beings thought in much the same way (Aristotelian) and should live in some past age (medieval or Baroque); church administration evaluated change as irrelevant or even evil.

Karl Rahner observed that, without history, religion degenerates into a spectacle at first watched and then imprisoning.

> This is true not only of the individual history of an individual person but also for the history of social units, of peoples and of the one human race. . . . The unity of mankind itself is not something fixed and unchangeable which moves through history but it too has a history. The supernatural existential has a history.[1]

Rahner showed how Catholic theology could accept the presence of history so that Jesus and his teaching remain at work and the Incarnation is not rendered transient or relative. Belief and justice, prayer or liturgy exist within several histories: the history of a person, the history of God's revelation and grace, and the history of Jesus and that of the Christian community. The following pages look at human and saving histories.

I. EXISTENTIAL HISTORY

God created people on planet Earth in time. Time is one of God's creatures. Human beings have been fashioned so as to be permeated by time. German thinkers from Schelling to Thomas Mann and Heidegger have described how the passing of the present into the past bestows life, and how in societies time gives existence and culture. In God's plan, some developmental dynamic leads on through billions of years and millions of species to the human person. The evolutionary process leads to the human being, whose knowledge and freedom draw natural history into cultural history. Time has its teleology, its goals, its purpose. Human beings come into existence to pursue science and art. They also receive in time a share in a higher life from God.

> The human world is freely called through time towards God's own life, in such a way that eternal value is concretely at issue in all the struggles of life. Through the passage of time, with its achievements and its losses, we become the persons and societies whom God has created as a body ready for holy anointing.[2]

Theology need not reexpress Christianity in a solely evolutionary pattern, but it should draw out the themes of history, development, and evolution that have been developed by Christianity from its first centuries, perspectives that stand in contrast to a static mechanism.[3]

Human history is long. Time allows the divine depth, the extent of grace to become human in religion, for the divine uses the objective, the categorical, to say to men and women something about itself. *Hearer of the Word* observed that God, if there was to be a revelation of a special life, would enter into human history. "Salvation history as such must belong to the dimension we call the history of humanity in a very objective and real sense."[4] History pervades God's offered salvation from Moses to Jesus, and from thousands of centuries before Moses. While the length and the future of history are not fully seen by people, faith holds that Jesus has announced something of them. Human history is not blotted out by saving history. Salvation is historical; grace accepts the temporal; religion changes as people change. The Bible records a segment of the history of God's revelation, and God's silent love of human beings does not avoid but embraces history.

II. SALVATION HISTORY AND WORLD HISTORY

Believers and theologians call a special presence of God "revelation" (in terms of ideas) or "grace" (in terms of empowerment) or "covenant" (in terms of community). God's personal love touches people in a temporal world of a lengthy past and an incipient future.

God and History. People and societies change. Does God change? Does a revelation, an action on earth from God, imply alteration in God? This is a popular topic of academic studies on religion. Does not God, like us, change, progress, suffer? Patristic and medieval theologies, attributing a sublime stasis to the Infinite and aware that God does not exist within the temporality of planet Earth, were cool toward change in God (they were not tempted by a modern sensitivity hoping to be consoled by a suffering divinity). That God is beyond our cycle of birth and death seems obvious. Yet, precisely the Christian belief in a Trinity and an Incarnation suggests some slight facet of alteration.

> It remains inevitably true that the Logos *became* man, that the changing history of this human reality is *his* own history: our time became the time of the eternal, our death the death of the immortal God himself. . . . We must simply say that God can become who is unchangeable in himself can *himself* become something, he who is unchangeable in himself can himself become subject to change *in something else.*[5]

Christianity can hardly ignore this issue, for the center of its faith—incarnation and grace in people—implies some entry into history. In spite of his immutability, God can become that creature he loves. This is not a sign of deficiency but of power. Salvation history is God's temporal place of grace. "God can become something, he who is changeable in himself can himself become subject to change *in something* else."[6] Why should not the power of God, enabling and loving the universe from the beginning of time, extend throughout time? God can enter time as he wishes, and the Bible states that God's special love does occur in history. The grace of God no longer comes down from on high, from a God transcending the world and without history, in episodes; it is in the world, in tangible historical forms. Nonetheless, any alteration in God lies within the sovereign otherness of his being and is a very minor aspect of God's work. "You can conceive of the world and its history as if gracious and saving interventions of God continually descend upon it from above, or you can think of it in such a way that the self-communicating God is its innermost heart."[7]

A Long History. Religions speak of origins, of mythological times. Christianity offers a revelation in history; it leads the beginnings of Israel to a fulfilling climax in the New Adam, Jesus. History is not a particular area for Christian reflection but the dynamic moving through the entire Bible, and key moments mark a history of God's special love. When God is understood as an Ultimate but also as loving and wise, and when grace is understood as offered to every human being, the beginning of history will be the beginning of a saving history, no matter how long ago.

> What we call God's grace is primarily . . . the self-communication of God in the depth of the person's spiritual existence. Now this self-communication is not something that, in the course of human history, happens only here and there sporadically. . . . But it is something that is, as a matter of course, offered always and everywhere to all human beings, whether they freely accept or reject it. . . . And this is the most fundamental, the most original element of what we call revelation.[8]

All salvation is salvation history, and Jesus Christ appears in a human history that is long. "But if we did get out of this habit (of overlooking the long spans of time) one thing would be clear for us: the whole biblical age from Abraham to Christ shrinks into a brief moment."[9]

The divine presence is everywhere seeking to direct, in silence and then in human words and actions, human life.

> Then you have from the very beginning a conception of history that involves a universal and supernatural revelation . . . , a history rendered dynamic through grace and finalized in a future planned by that same self-communication of God.[10]

Without history, God's presence would be static and monoform.

Today theology gives attention to each individual life, accepts the extent of salvation history, and interprets both in light of the Incarnation. The Christian needs to understand the relationship of dynamic grace to personality and society. One must flee three theoretical extremes: human history without Christ; Christ as a dim light for a few in a vast world and history of condemnation; or Christ as one of many religious founders. The reign of God is present from the beginning of time as earth's destiny and as a redemption for all. "God is seen as the one who creates what is other than himself in order precisely to communicate himself to it. In this view the history of revelation and the history of the world, while not simply identical are always and everywhere co-existent."[11] In the history of religions, mystics and prophets point to Trinity and Incarnation and Resurrection, although these remain glimpsed but not fully known. His writings on the self-transcendence of the human toward mystery are an exaltation of the person and an opening toward a wider universe.

> The highest point of its development evolves into spirit, once again actually moves beyond itself (in what is called grace and glory) toward an immediacy to the absolute God, then that can be understood, even when it is nothing more than a datum of revelation, as a prolongation of the world's evolution which, through the power of God himself, tends toward that spirit which has an immediacy to God himself. In a world of evolution of this kind matter cannot be conceived as a mere launching pad which is left behind, or the first stage of a movement which is simply cast off. The dogma of the resurrection of the body prevents the Christian thinker from subscribing to this idea.[12]

The Incarnation is not deduced from progress nor does it reject all evolution and development. There is an affinity between history and forms of development and the presence of Word and Spirit in a history of salvation.

III. JESUS CHRIST

Although grace is present through hundreds of thousands of years, Christians believe in a central teaching and efficacy given by Jesus Christ. Jesus as the Christ makes explicit God's plan for humanity. That history of revelation comes to its climax when the divine self-communication becomes a human being, Jesus of Nazareth. In him, the divine being who expresses (God), the mode of expression (the human reality of the man of Nazareth), and the recipient (Jesus as a graced prophet) have become one individual. Jesus the Christ is not the strict teacher of precise ecclesiastical laws and dogmas, but a primal force in humanity; he does not bring to a small community a few moments of salvation, but rather elevates humanity, religion, by grace.[13] Jesus is the special image of God, God's picture or icon interpreting the history of grace in human history and its triumphant future.

> In Jesus the human question and God's answer have become one, not confounded and undivided. In him God and humanity are one without

suppressing the other. In Jesus God as the unutterable mystery has totally
and irrevocably expressed the divine as Word; in him the Word is present
as spoken to all of us by the God of nearness, inexpressible intimacy, and
forgiveness.[14]

Jesus intensifies that presence of God to a high power, making its transcendental form explicit. The structures of Jesus' personality are the means, the vital channels for revelation and life. In that history of God's outreach of love, the Logos becomes most categorical in an individual living on earth.

The Word does not live in Jesus of Nazareth gingerly and briefly, disdaining the material and the human, the social and historical. The Word out of love has taken on in Jesus our humanity and our world. "God is in the place where we are and he gazes at us in a human being."[15] Can a Christian speak appropriately of God unless at the same time he or she speaks of the human person? Rahner's theology of God touching the human subject and history appears in the narrative of Jesus of Nazareth. God becomes a human being so that human beings can share in God's life, of the self-transcending openness of the depth of being-human. Through the teaching and death and resurrection of Jesus, the Word enters history and seeks to explain and direct it.

In patristic christologies, the Word's presence in one human being is an affirmation and presence of God in every human being. The incarnation of God is the highest case of the realization of the human person. Jesus, as Son of God, unfolds the mystery of being-a-human and the mystery of being-God's-Word. The transcendental reality of grace looks not to an idealist system, a psychology or a mythology, but to actions and teachings of the incarnate Word. "Every person lives necessarily in an order of existence which includes the reality of Christ."[16] The Incarnation is unique and intense, but it builds upon past presences of grace and expands out to touch the entire human family.

Jesus lived in his religious world; he tried to reform it and then saw that the reform was destined for all people and would endanger his life; with increasing clarity he preached the invitation and the mandate of the kingdom of God. His message led to his death, but that death led to resurrection. Jesus, Rahner points out, lives in a world. With humanity for his world, Jesus acts within the world, that is, in the histories of billions of lives.

> Now Christianity cannot let go of the claim both to have received the
> definitive and all-embracing word of grace in Jesus, crucified and risen,
> and to preach this still to the world today. But this is not to deny that the

liberating Spirit of God is active in all finite human affairs, within every perplexity and error. The non-Christian world religions witness in their own fashion not only to human limitation but also the Spirit of Jesus.[17]

Faith faces the challenge that the birth of Jesus is far in the past, and that it is an event at the end and at the beginning of hundreds of thousands of years, and yet it is the reality, the sacrament, the milieu of the Word of God. The narratives of Jesus do not indicate that the kingdom touches only a small group of the saved cut off from billions of sinners. The gospel's good news is not glorified by becoming the bad news for other people. The originality and scandal of his teaching is that God's love is inclusive. How this works backwards in time, and how it effects people who could not know Jesus, is a difficult issue. Rahner recognized the difficulty in linking the grace of the Spirit given in all times and places and the historical event of Calvary and space. He introduced as a complement to the traditional causality of the Cross a final causality of the risen Christ and his Spirit coming from the future. The Holy Spirit is the cause of the Incarnation and so the mission of Jesus and his goal are born by the Spirit.

> He is from the beginning the Spirit of Jesus Christ. Insofar as this Spirit always and everywhere brings justifying faith, this faith is always and everywhere and from the outset a faith which comes to be in the Spirit of Jesus Christ. In this Spirit of his, he [Jesus] is present and operative in all faith.[18]

To ask how the historical Jesus who is the risen Christ influences those who do not know or accept him is a mysterious issue but it is not new: it is the same issue as asking how the grace of Calvary works on those living prior to that event. Rahner's response is that the Spirit of Jesus is the agent of a wider grace. Rahner describes how Jesus is present to those who have not heard of him in his mode of Spirit, the Holy Spirit, the Spirit of the risen Christ. "The Spirit is always, everywhere and from the outset the entelechy, the determining principle, of the history of revelation and salvation."[19] David Coffey concludes:

> For Rahner the Holy Spirit has the role of "Spirit of Christ" even before the Incarnation, namely as "entelechy" directed to the Christ event. Before, and in preparation for the Son's historical return to the Father, in Christ, the Spirit, precisely as entelechy, has to seek him in history, that is through the creation and evolution of the cosmos, the arrival of humans, the consequent and new operation of the Spirit as grace, and the history of Israel culminating in the lives of Mary and, finally, in Jesus, in whom this operation finds its goal. This Spirit then assumes various roles as the

Spirit of Jesus during the Messiah's lifetime and afterwards in the church. "This continues even after the Incarnation, in leading to Christ (as 'anonymous Christians') men and women of goodwill, including those belonging to the world religions."[20]

Rahner's interest in Jesus' life (shown in books of meditations and prayers, in sermons for the feasts of the liturgical year) flows from a concern that any presentation of Christ for contemporary believers be concrete. During his life and mission, Jesus himself comes to a full consciousness of the nature of his role; he is the eschatological prophet, the absolute and definitive Savior. The Word of God and the religious prophet illumine each other. The presence of the Logos in a Jewish prophet unfolds in what the four Gospels narrate, and the divine Word speaks and works through the existential and cultural life of Jesus of Nazareth who is not an object to be isolated in a heavenly glow, but a door, a portal into the mystery of divine presence and human life.[21] Andreas Batlogg sums up his study of Rahner's consideration of the life of Christ in this way:

> With Jesus, the human person as a *Hearer of the Word* becomes a *Seer of the Word.* . . . The mysteries of the life of Jesus in the interpretation of Rahner's fundamental theology could give a new access for faith. . . . Drawn deeply into the life of Jesus the human person experiences her own transitions and transformations. Jesus takes the person by the hand and accompanies him through life.[22]

There is, however, still much for Christians to ponder when asked about future fulfillment, about the process of how Jesus the Christ will save all humanity. The human person is drawn by the light of the future and by questions of meaning posed by death to seek what is given explicitly in Christ.[23]

The incarnate Word who is the definitive prophet of religion finds his fulfillment in a death that is a breakthrough to life, resurrection.

> The incarnation is not merely the constituting of a subject who, if eventually he is willing or is given the task by God, can intercede for sinful mankind before the holy majesty of God. . . . Rather, God by the incarnation took the world fundamentally and once and for all into his mercy. Through the incarnation the whole of redemption was already pre-formed, even if it still had to be carried out in that suffering of death. . . . Consequently the whole of humanity is in principle already accepted for salvation in this member and head of humanity who is irrevocably united with God in the unity of the person.[24]

Jesus shows the historically real and active presence of the victorious
mercy of God in the future. Jesus' death is not a mishap or an unexpected
attack. As the gospels narrate, Jesus' provocative teaching leads to rejection; fidelity to the Father's teaching brings public execution. Faith and
hope and love appear in an eminent way, in a death inspiring each person.
Rahner employs Heidegger's insights to explain the role death plays in
the totality of a life. Death has active and passive dimensions; it is the end
of biological life and (even more) a delivery into the all-disposing power
of God. Death is not an accident but a resolution of life, a transition to
another life, not so much the end of an organism but a change in existence. Amid social and religious condemnation on Calvary, Jesus' death
is human and prophetic and redemptive. What persons in faith accept
freely in their death reflects the direction of their life born by the grace of
Christ. Jesus' acceptance of the Good Thief shows death leads to life.

> By freely accepting the fate of death Jesus surrenders himself precisely to
> the unforeseen and incalculable possibilities of his existence. . . . The
> life and death of Jesus, or the death which recapitulates and culminates his
> life, possess a causality of a quasi-sacramental and real-symbolic nature.
> In this causality what is signified, in this case God's salvific will, posits the
> sign, in this case the death of Jesus along with his resurrection.[25]

Death is a passage for Jesus, a personal and a collective passage. Jesus'
death and resurrection draw his life forward. They are not two distinct
events but go together as do death (an existential of life and a place for
grace to triumph) and the entry into eternal life. The unique presence
of the Logos in one human subject draws all other lives to Jesus. Life
and death on earth are not separate from the person who lived.[26] Each
person's existence passes into death, and, faith holds, then into resurrection. The resurrection comes to a human person who has lived on
earth in the totality of a life: it does not mean an idea or reincarnation
or a soul separated from corporeal life.

> Cross and Resurrection belong together in a real mature faith in Jesus.
> Cross proclaims an unveiled demand of unconditional capitulation of
> the human person before the mystery of his existence, a recognition
> that he is not in control of a life of finitude and guilt, while resurrec-
> tion means the content of unconditional hope that in this dying brings
> forgiveness and blessed and definitive acceptance of this human being
> through the mystery of resurrection, at a moment where letting go no
> longer holds any fear of falling.[27]

IV. THE WORD OF JESUS CHRIST: THE BIBLE

Karl Rahner's theology draws on patristic and medieval, Baroque and modern theologies, philosophies, and spiritualities. Is it odd, even presumptuous to think that this theology has much to do with Scripture? Surely its philosophical conceptuality has pushed the New Testament aside. Rahner is not an exegete, and yet he intended to explain what was most basic in the New Testament. Books and articles, sermons and meditations thought through and gave vital expression to the biblical message. Human history of encounters with God lie beneath the books of the Bible expressed in their literary forms. There is an unavoidable and justified task in asking about the meaning of the Bible, about what is the reality being expressed in books that are at times poetic.

The New Testament. The salvific will of God, the redemptive death of Jesus, salvation history, the love of neighbor, are biblical themes serving as principles for theology. "The New Testament must be understood as an expression in writing of an already reflective early Christianity which is directly anchored to the historical Jesus."[28] The human being as an event of the presence of God in history[29] is at the center of the New Testament writings. The opening theme of the New Testament is the approach of holy mystery, coming near, near to all. That revelation draws the existence of people to Jesus who, in his daily life and ministry, is teacher, model, and promise.[30] Jesus' teaching begins with the concrete and existential, with the religious mentality and movements of the times. With Jesus, a new dynamic of what was already present arrived on earth with more power. The kingdom of God is, in the modern philosophical language of Rahner, ontological, that is, real and existential, personal and historical. Since that reign is radically of God, only story, insight, metaphor, and simile can try to explain a world of love, forgiveness, justice, and future life. Jesus refuses to quantify religious rituals or to reduce life in the Spirit to commercial exchange.

The Jesuit differs from Protestant liberal theologians: for over a century they have tried to attract the modern person to Christianity by reducing the supernatural message of the New Testament, locating the divine in human self-transcendence, psychological growth, or aesthetic drives of our personality. The supranatural is unacceptable in the modern world. A bias against the suprahuman rejects God intervening in history: concrete forms and dogmas (categorical realizations of Christianity with their limits and possible corruptions) are primitive and superstitious religion. Rahner is far from this: the intervention of God is primary, and the forms of church life can be sacramental.[31]

One biblical facet running through Rahner's theology is the dynamics of love. The Gospels join the love of God with love of self and neighbor. Love of neighbor and love of God go together.[32] Loving one's neighbor is not an arbitrary religious mandate or ideal, something Christians must do because it is difficult. "The love of God unreflectedly but really and always intends God in supernatural transcendentality in the love of neighbor. . . . The act by which the neighbor is loved is really the primal (even if still non-explicit) act by which God is loved."[33] The incarnate Word in a man is the source and affirmation of the two loves: God's love for humanity overflows into God becoming one of us.[34] Jesus becoming a human being is the most daring and serious affirmation of the value of men and women, "a never reversed acceptance of humanity by the Logos."[35] God loves human beings enough to become one, and so men and women should respect one another. In loving God (who is the Word as a human being), we love the other. We love others, all others, not because of God's command but because of God's presence in his images who are now the brothers and sisters of the incarnate Word called to resurrection. "If the Scripture says that someone who loves the neighbor has fulfilled the law this is the ultimate truth because God has become this neighbor and so in every neighbor that one who is closest and most distant at the same time is always received and loved."[36] Love of God and love of neighbor revealed in incarnation are one, a structure of reality, and these loves flow from their awareness of a common origin and ground.

The Gospel according to Matthew. One finds similarities between Karl Rahner's theology and the Gospel according to Matthew. Jesus preaches the "kingdom of God," a realm of mercy and love and justice, a source of religious life that is honest and interior. In describing God's kingdom, Jesus remains within the transcendental mode, illustrating what cannot easily be prescribed in religious things but is described in stories and illustrations. Although asked to give concrete limits to what he means by "neighbor" and "mercy," he does not choose numbers or laws to delineate behavior, and refuses categorical answers about religious rites and obligations.

The reign of God exists in an invisible and silent mode, and yet it is real and active, powerful and normative. This realm is the source and critic of religion, of temple and church. Teaching within the traditions of Judaism, Jesus nonetheless stands at times outside any specific religion, indeed outside human religion itself. The fifth chapter of the Gospel according to Matthew, the Sermon on the Mount, leads the hearers from external religion to an interior orientation, one human and divine. It is not what one eats that is a sign of religiosity but "what comes out of the mouth proceeds from the heart" (15:17). Those who are strict with externals often ignore what is human and holy, "transgressing the commandment of God" for the sake of human tradition" (15:3). Not the objects of religion but the inner and ethical behavior of people concerns God: "I desire mercy not sacrifice" (9:13; 12:7). In a climactic and revolutionary moment, the Messiah proclaims that he and his teaching about religion and kingdom are above all religion: "the Son of Man is Lord of the Sabbath" (12:7). There is here a considerable critique of religion. The outward display of clothes and rituals hides the interior selfishness. Still, external observances of a religion are not rejected by a Puritanism but are criticized so that they might lead to what lies within God and humanity and beneath all forms and institutions, and one religion is not replaced by another. Externals and regulations are judged by how they sustain a giving heart. Categorical realizations may present grace, and they, too, can have a positive form drawn from existential and cultural history, capable of transformation and renewal.

Jesus pays attention to the existential situation of each man and woman who comes to him. A Roman centurion does not have much theological or religious knowledge, and his ideas and rituals may be on the surface erroneous, but the orientation of his person is filled with grace. A woman who is not Jewish becomes through Jesus' clever pedagogy a theological instructor to the Messiah, teaching him that his mission is not just for Jews. He is interested in someone's faith and commitment to the values of the kingdom of God. It is not those who have the correct phrases ("Lord, Lord") who manifest that commitment, but those who follow God's plan: better an act of mercy than a discussion of theology.

In religion, no scene is more important than the drama of the end of the world, the final judgment on individual life. Curiously, in Jesus' dramatic narrative at the end of the Gospel according to Matthew, people are judged not by religious ideas and rituals but by their human treatment of others. What is significant in human and graced life is rather anonymous. A human life responding to divine grace is manifest in actions of help, of help toward the most needy: that assistance need not be given a religious dress or interpretation. No lack of exegetes find that in Matthew (25:31-46) "the criterion according to which judgment is made to lie solely and exclusively with mercy to other men and women, for Christ calls those who live from this mercy 'the blessed of his Father' and he welcomes them into his kingdom."[37] Rahner employs here the reality of love.

> Many have met Jesus Christ unawares, not realizing that they have grasped someone into whose life and death a man or woman plunges as into a blessed redeeming destiny. God and the grace of Christ are in everything as the secret essence of every chosen reality, and so it is not easy to grasp something and to avoid any contact with God or grace.[38]

The teaching of Jesus in the four Gospels is an effort to describe God's gift for all people and to go beneath religion to God as its source and standard, to go beyond human religion to the reign of God.

New Testament Letters. To turn to other New Testament writings, a transcendental primacy for God and grace is found in chapter eight of Paul's letter to the Romans, where the gift of God is "the law of the spirit of life in Christ Jesus" (8:2). This law is not rules but an inexpressible yet real mode or realm of existence, the life of the Holy Spirit. Rahner's theology can be seen as a reflection on this chapter of Romans when it states that the Spirit of the risen Christ dwells in a believer. The letter to the Hebrews finds a breadth in salvation history and locates the life and death of Jesus amid human religion.

R. P. Meyer compared Rahner's theology with the letter to the Ephesians. Both emphasize the goodness of God active in his plan, in the mystery of what he has thought out for humanity. Ephesians centers God's plan for human salvation on Christ, and yet it is clear that the plan is broader and earlier than Bethlehem. Salvation comes not just to a few souls but to the human family, and the conviction that all are objectively saved in Christ leads to a theology of the Holy Spirit as a further mode and manifestation of the Word as risen Christ. The human person is called to realize the life of the Logos in the presence of the Holy Spirit. The power of this plan for the human family has layers in a world where God draws people to a life patterned after the divine life, a plan of salvation having its climax, if not its temporal beginning, in Jesus of Nazareth, a fullness generously offered to all peoples. Both the Pauline letter and modern theology take as their themes a missionary expansion of grace in terms of diversity and history. "The providence of salvation consists in God's irrevocable and universal will of salvation, in a grace without borders, and that is also a consequence of the theology of *Ephesians*."[39] The church is a charismatic and missionary proclamation of the plan for people, a community not of a few fixed offices but of a variety of ministries.

For Rahner, the goal of exegesis is making lucid the teaching of Jesus, and theology is not a flight from Scripture but its explanation.[40] Is Jesus mainly a teacher of information about a deity? Does he bring new rituals and new remedies for vice? In fact, he interprets what is happening in each individual living between sin and grace. There is little indication that the New Testament is teaching a narrow, automatic condemnation of all those who could not have heard, geographically or existentially, about the centrality of Jesus.[41] The personal emphasis on Scripture is quite contemporary.

V. GOD'S WIDE LOVE AND LIFE

Jesus proclaimed himself to be God's word in a unique way: he is for all the light of the world. At times of geographical discovery, cross-cultural encounters, and global awareness, those who confess Jesus Christ will ask: What is the relationship of their faith in a unique savior to the enormous population of men and women, past and present, who could not know about him? When the Christian church was entering the culture of the Greco-Roman world, theologians only a century or so after Pentecost recognized this problem: how was truth and grace from the Word Incarnate related to human religion and philosophy? Later Christians, in ages of exploration during the thirteenth and sixteenth centuries, learned of large populations with no awareness of Jesus.

Theologies of faith and grace outside baptism and explicit belief have existed for centuries. The eucharistic prayers of the Mass pray "for all who have left this world in your friendship." Vespers in the first week in Advent begins that time of meditation on the Incarnation with the words, "Lord, be mindful of all men [and women], who from the beginning of time have placed their trust in you," while on Good Friday, the Solemn Intercessory Prayers ask that "those who do not believe in Christ" might have "the light of the Holy Spirit show them the way to salvation." These views had their origins in theologies of the Logos in the third century, and in the theology of Thomas Aquinas and his commentators. Members of other religions can have an implicit faith in and a forward-moving intention toward values Jesus taught. Some Protestant theologies may hold that such religions are perverse, corrupt, devilish (this negative Anglo-Saxon fear of world religions appeared in the movies of the 1940s where a temple, a statue in some exotic land is a frightening place of evil). The Jesuit theologian had first developed a perspective of wider grace to explain how modern Europeans who had left an arrogant or irrelevant church for a movement that hoped to improve human life (socialism, Marxism) might have not given up God's friendship. Rahner's theory of wider grace has its origins in a pastoral concern we all have, about relatives and children who leave the church; later, it moves on to a wider form, world religions.[42]

In the 1960s, thanks to the end of European colonialism, the emergence of new nations, the expansion of a global economy, and jet travel and electronic communications, the world began to come together in a global reality, and business executives and tourists met devout Hindus and Muslims in their particular religious worlds considering life and death, goodness and pain. In 1961 a first essay on "Christianity and the Non-Christian Religions" asked: Do people's religions only hold the morally corrupt and the religiously demonic? Rahner gave a global context and a modern expression to the traditional Catholic theology of wider grace.

God's love comes to each human being even if the realities of Trinity and Incarnation cannot be known. The free act of a believer involves the entire person and aims at some further fullness; God searches out and empowers each person, no matter how sinful or secular they might be (as the image of the Good Shepherd exemplifies). There can be an authentic life of grace among those whose historical situation makes it impossible for them to know of or be existentially interested in Christ, a life of grace having its own visibility. The self-sharing of God comes prior to Jewish prophecy and Christian church into the depths of each person from Adam and Eve on, and so always and everywhere history is salvation history.

> The one who, therefore, no matter how far they are from explicit verbal formulations of revelation accepts existence, accepts one's humanity in silent patience (in faith, hope, and love—whatever they are called) accepts it as the mystery which hides in itself the mystery of eternal love and bears in the core of death life, that person says, 'Yes' to something that is such a mystery. For it has trusted itself to this One in a mode without measure, and God has filled with what is immeasurable, that is, with God's self. . . .[43]

God's self-revelation in the depths of the spiritual person is a certain atmosphere in which the human person lives.

> Since this grace from God is offered to all people in all ages for Christ's sake (and in its being-offered is efficacious) and (we may hope, though it is impossible to know for certain) at least the majority of people accept it (even when they are unable to reflect on this event happening in the inmost core of their spiritual person) to the extent this grace alters a human's consciousness.[44]

Rahner here sets aside the old textbook explanation that, while grace was offered to the nonbaptized, it was weak, inefficacious, impotent. There are not different kinds of grace with a second-rate form given to those who are not Christians. One grace touched by social life and religion is at work within the important decisions of each life.

> To some extent, human questioning is filled through this ineffable, divine self-communication (to us) with the confident faith that God answers the infinite question with the infinite answer that is himself; through this grace, always and already, a self-revelation of God as a free, gracious event is given at all times. Thus, always and everywhere, history is the history of salvation and of revelation.[45]

As we have seen, as the history of grace holds a message and a power, the history of grace is revelatory.

> God's self-revelation in the depths of the spiritual person is a certain depth of knowing (in the transcendental-psychological and not emotional sense) produced by grace. This history of reflection forms an intrinsic part of the historical process of God's self-disclosure in grace because this self-disclosure possesses an inherent dynamism that urges it to objectify itself.[46]

God is not an irritable and irritated watcher of people down on earth whose interventions are more or less doomed to failure. People with their religions manifest God's silent presence moving in history. The one process of salvation is "a history which God governs and which is therefore, a further divine revelation."[47] One can maintain Christianity's claim to be the culmination of the graced contact by God with humanity verbally and sacramentally without denying that men and women who do not lock God out by personal viciousness are saved.

Protestant critics have spoken of the "arrogance" of Rahner's theology, locating all men and women in God's grace. Is a worldview in which God loves all condescending? Would people prefer to be told that Christians believe they are neglected or condemned by God? Actually, it is an enormous presumption for an individual to decide that another human being is hated and abandoned by God, for every man and woman and child is the icon of the incarnate Word and a neighbor whom we are invited to love. The misery and exclusion of others are not needed to glorify the Light of the World. This theology treats the extent of grace and not the limits of the church. Catholic tradition sees the church as people on the rolls of parishes, and an affirmation of a wider presence of grace does not involve a pretended or implicit membership in the Catholic Church (the misdirection of a few theologians after 1880 and of Pius XII) but of belonging to the reign of God.

Grace is a basic theme of Rahner from the beginning, and the extent of grace in time past, present, and future remains a theme and a lasting accomplishment.

VI. PEOPLE'S RELIGIONS

What makes divine love concrete may not always be explicitly Christian (although Christians should be ready to show how entry into the church brings advantages). Members of religions, living honestly and even selflessly in moments of inward reflection and silent service to others, live in what Jesus called God's kingdom. As Jesus taught during his encounters with non-Jews, those who have little connection to organized religion may have "the pearl of great price," a graced life, while arrogant officials of religion may be deluding themselves. Religions embrace more than sporadic and occasional acts toward religious things, and they seek in different places at various times to interpret the human drama engaged with God. There is no lack of human aspects of religion that are perverse and violent, but not all human religion is ugly.

> In principle the attempt is made in every religion (at least on the human adherents' part) to interpret explicitly original, non-reflexive, non-objectified revelation and to express it in the form of propositions. And in every religion we find isolated instances of successful reflection, reflection made possible by the divine grace whereby God gives people (even in the dimension of objectivity and concrete historicity) an opportunity for salvation. But as God permits human sin in general and this obscures and corrupts every dimension of human life, individual and social, so the history of human attempts to objectify revelation is not excepted. The attempt is only partially successful, and revelation is mingled with error and culpable ignorance.[48]

Every religious history seeks to explain the paradigm of grace, sin, and people; and religions have more in common with each other than with agnostic or sinful rejections of anything beyond human life.

Rahner referred to "subjective religion" as the presence and offer of grace, the entry into a person at various levels of the dynamic of divine revelation and life. Religion begins not with a prophet or a rite of initiation but with the interior reality of God's love. "Objective religion" is the realization in cult and teaching of sin and salvation and has a cultural and social dimension. "Religion means the transcendental dimension being expressed, being expressed in a concrete way [of grace and revelation] in knowledge and free decision."[49] Objectively, a religion is not equal to the explicit revelation the Christian church preaches and makes concrete. "It is not the non-Christian religions as historically concrete systems or institutions which are ways to salvation for their members. Rather, the way of salvation of the individual person as a saving way is drawn basically from the subject."[50]

As the decades passed, Rahner went beyond this too subjective theology of salvation (produced by a church metaphysics from the 1920s) to inquire into grace in religion. If God's grace in religion remains unclear, the self-communication of God cannot reach billions of human beings devoted to their religion while disdaining religion. So not all religions from God's point of view are something tolerated, bypassed, marginalized. Not a student of Asian or African religions, he did not begin with a comparison of rituals but with the Christian conviction that God reveals himself universally to people and their histories. Rahner was a Catholic theologian looking at the vast phenomenon of religion from the perspective of faith in Jesus Christ as the central revelation of God for men and women, a Christian asking about the limitations, the power, and the future of what Christianity professes. Theology should give a positive view of Christianity toward religion. Can the religious milieu of an individual touched by grace be, a priori, excluded from grace? This theology lets the forms and ideas of religions appear in their own world (although eventually measured against Jesus' teaching). Christians are not an arbitrary, preselected part of the human family in a world in which the accidents of birth determine potential salvation.

> The basis for considering the relationship of religions to Christianity is the theology of grace. . . . He interprets the general will of God to save in terms of people in non-Christian religions . . . , enabling such an explanation through the concept of "the supernatural existential" which underlies the theory of "the anonymous Christian."[51]

Despite falsehood, misdirection, and depravation, religions in varying degree can be legitimate ways of salvation. Religions are ways of people following their consciences, ways of worship, words, and colors pointing toward the realities of Jesus' kingdom of God. God's grace makes them to be paths of salvation on which people meet God and his Christ.

> A Christian recognizes every person in the ultimate depths of his conscience, of his person and of his existence as someone to whom the infinite, nameless and indefinable God, who is the true content of every spiritual life, has offered himself as salvation to the freedom of this person . . . [even when] this person interprets his existence without fault

in a different way or in a non-Christian way, perhaps even in an atheistic way.[52]

In the modern centuries, Christians, perhaps influenced by the Enlightenment, have preferred to see religions as a collection of ideas and rites to be analyzed by academic lectures shying away from concrete external manifestations of religion (liturgy, mysticism, monasticism). A narrow European ideology saw Christianity as a preselected part of the human species in a world in which accidents of birth reflected an unpredictable divine will bestowing and withholding salvation. God and his kingdom is greater than any religion or church. The Logos has already been in the world prior to Bethlehem. Jesus' teaching is everywhere the source of what religious consciousness seeks to express. Salvation history is not a brief time in sordid human history taking place around the Mediterranean, but a dynamic whose ground is the Holy Spirit. Early theologians taught that the pluralism of cultures and philosophies in the Roman Empire leads to and is illumined by the entry of the Logos. Vatican II's optimistic view of grace in the world and outside Christianity—Rahner noted the lack of controversy over it in the discussions of the council—had been a remarkable decision, a bold step forward. Personal engagement with religions brings realism, contacts with their experiences of sin and grace. The pluralism of religions comes from cultures and religious viewpoints, for God's plan and message moving through millennia exceeds what can be uncovered by one religion.

Going further, Rahner posed an important and difficult question for Christians. Does only the Hebrew covenant lead to Jesus' teaching and realization of the reign of God? Or, "do other various histories of religion arising in different places in the world and at different times in the history of the human race?"[53] Religions are not the same. Religions are not neutral: some might oppose Christian teaching, some might implicitly resemble it, some might have similarities. The Bible teaches that the entire human family (and so all religion) stands under the wisdom of God, and some of what is instructive in the history of Israel happens in other peoples. Consequently, what we call a special salvation history leading to the central climactic figure of Jesus "could also have taken place and has taken place in the history of other peoples."[54] Some religions might be anticipatory and influential in salvation history. Rahner distinguished between a general salvation history, where grace touches all over a million years, and a less than special history reaching from Abraham to Jesus. If religions, too, have grace and some direction by God, are all religions except Judaism and Christianity (as he held) limited to general salvation history? Could other religions be special in salvation history, leading in an important way, not to the birth of the Messiah, but to the future coming of Jesus? Salvation history is viewed as a continuum with two components, Judaism and Christianity, and yet that continuum does not quite exist: Judaism continues to live, and Christianity has churches and theologies with elements from Germanic or African religions. Christianity could emerge out of religions whose figures and ideas prepare for the reign of God, as emerged from Logos and Torah.

> Why should there not be events in the [wider] history of salvation and revelation which have analogous character analogous to the Jews? Why should there not be elsewhere in the history of humanity religions that are bearers of religious impulses . . . similar to the covenant with Israel with its prophets, religious institutions, holy scriptures?[55]

Why is the role of precursor to the definitive, explicit revelation of God's person and plan limited to Israel?

God's grace has an incarnational structure: it does not shy away from the human and the material. Trinity–Incarnation–Grace—these three central beliefs are facets of the one divine reality touching all history. While Christians believe Jesus is the dynamic center of the past, present, and future of grace, he can also be the fulfillment of millions of religious quests and of lines of worship whose goal they little glimpse. The centrality of Jesus Christ in a long history of religions, in a long history of humanity, and in a long history of the church—these are the issues for today and for the future.

NOTES

1. *F* 141.

2. O'Donovan, "A Journey into Time. The Legacy of Karl Rahner's Last Years," *TS* 46 (1985) 645. Rahner composed an article with Golo Mann, "Weltgeschichte und Heilsgeschichte," *Christlicher Glaube in moderner Gesellschaft* (Freiburg: Herder, 1978) 90–123.

3. See "Christology in the Setting of Modern Man's Understanding Himself and of His World, *TI* 11, 215–29; "Natural Science and Reasonable Faith," *TI* 16–55; Béla Weissmahr, "Selbstüberbietung und die Evolution des Kosmos auf Christus hin," in A. Raffelt, ed., *Karl Rahner in Erinnerung* (Düsseldorf: Patmos, 1994) 143–77.

4. *F* 240.

5. "On the Theology of the Incarnation," *TI* 4, 113; see Joseph Donceel, "Can our God never change?" *Theology Digest* 20 (1972) 207–12.

6. Ibid.

7. *KRD* 127.

8. *KRD* 75.

9. *F* 166.

10. *KRD* 127f.

11. *KRD* 127.

12. "Natural Science and Reasonable Faith," *TI* 21, 54. Rahner pursued, in a parallel way, the pattern developed by his fellow Jesuit Pierre Teilhard de Chardin with its principles of a long history, evolution, and development, the force of love, and the Christ as a magnet drawing humanity forward. "Rahner was deeply influenced by reading the writings of Teilhard de Chardin. Although he did not pursue special topics of Teilhard, he was inspired by his own theology of human evolution in the totality of the cosmos" *KRB* 105. "Above all Karl Rahner's transcendental theology is considereably inspired by Teilhard's ideas" (Alexander Loichinger, "Pierre Teilhard de Chardin [1881–1955]. Zum 50. Todestag," *Theologische Revue* 101 [2005] 120); see H. K. Kodikuthiyil, "Faith Engaged in Dialogue with Science. A Comparative Study of Pierre Teilhard de Chardin's and Karl Rahner's Reception of the Theory of Evolution" (Ph.D. dissertation, Catholic University of Leuven, 1998); Leo O'Donovan, "Der Dialog mit dem Darwinismus. Zur theologischen Verwendung des evolutiven Weltbilds bei Karl Rahner," *WT* 215–29.

13. "The One Christ and the Universality of Salvation," *TI* 16, 199–224.

14. "Understanding Christmas," *TI* 23, 144.

15. *Everyday Faith* (New York: Herder and Herder, 1968) 114; see J. M. McDermott, "The Christologies of Karl Rahner, I, II," *Gregorianum* 27 (1986) 87–123; 297–327. Xavier Tilliette notices how Rahner's theology illustrates the perdurance of a few directions from the christologies of the idealists like Schelling, always drawing them into history and existence (*La Christologie idéaliste* [Paris: Desclée, 1986] 217–21).

16. "Priestly Existence," *TI* 3, 297; see *F* 198.

17. "The Foundation of Belief," *TI* 16, 21; see *F* 247f.

18. *F* 318; see Morwenna Ludlow, *Universal Salvation. Eschatology in the Thought of Gregory of Nyssa and Karl Rahner* (Oxford: Oxford University Press, 2000).

19. *TI* 17, 46.

20. Coffey, "The Spirit of Christ as Entelechy," *Philosophy & Theology* 13 (2000) 363.

21. Herbert Vorgrimler, "Der Begriff der Selbsttranszendenz in der Theologie Karl Rahners," *WT* 253–58; see G. Lohaus, "Die Lebensereignisse Jesu in der Christologie Karl Rahners," *Theologie und Philosophie* 65 (1990) 349–86; on Rahner and Mary the mother of Jesus, see Karl Neufeld, "Zur Mariologie Karl Rahners. Materialien und Grundlinien," *Zeitschrift für katholische Theologie* 109 (1987) 431–9.

22. Andreas Batlogg, *Die Mysterien des Lebens Jesu bei Karl Rahner. Zugang zum Christusglauben* (Innsbruck: Tyrolia, 2003) 415f.

23. *F* 293f.; on Rahner's theology of Christ, both from human life and divine Trinity, see Harvey Egan, *Karl Rahner. Mystic of Everyday Life* (New York: Crossroad, 1998) 130–6.

24. *The Church and the Sacraments* (New York: Herder and Herder, 1963) 14.

25. *F* 255, 284; see *On the Theology of Death* (New York: Herder, 1965); "Ideas for a Christian Theology of Death," *TI* 13, 169–86. Rahner warned that sacrificial

terminology may encourage the inference that Jesus' death grudgingly effects a change in God rather than being itself an effect of God's love.

26. "Jesus' Resurrection," *TI* 17, 21ff.

27. "Warum bin ich heute ein Christ?" in Albert Raffelt, Karl Lehmann, eds., *Praxis des Glaubens* (Freiburg: Herder, 1982) 30. "[Jesus'] resurrection is like the first eruption of a volcano which shows that in the interior of the world God's fire is already burning, and this will bring everything to blessed ardor in his light. . . . Already from the heart of the world into which he descended in death, the new forces of a transfigured earth are at work." "A Faith That Loves the Earth," *Everyday Faith* (New York: Herder and Herder, 1968) 80f.; on death and life in christology, see Andreas Batlogg, *Die Mysterien,* 350–8.

28. *KRD* 228; see Rudolf Pesch, "Gegen eine doppelte Wahrheit. Karl Rahner und die Bibelwissenschaft," in *LGG* 10–36.

29. This is the title of chapter 4 of *Foundations.* Trying to show that New Testament theologies develop something like a transcendental christology is Karl Rahner and Wilhelm Thüsing, *A New Christology* (New York: Seabury, 1980).

30. See Andreas Batlogg, *Die Mysterien,* 360–80.

31. See *KRD* 312–5; Michael B. Raschko, "Karl Rahner and Demythologization," *TS* 56 (1995) 551–5; Vorgrimler concluded that this theology is "never reduction, and always concentration" ("Grundzüge der Theologie Karl Rahners. Zugleich ein Blick auf seine bleibende Aktualität," in *Karl Rahner. Sehnsucht nach dem geheimnisvollen Gott* [Freiburg: Herder, 1990] 39).

32. "I consider this thesis of Rahner to be one of the most important and seminal of recent theology which in fact has for understanding Christianity today 'epochal significance'" (Helmut Peukert, "Kommunikative Freiheit und absolute befreiende Freiheit," *WT* 281). Comparing Rahner with some contemporary exegetes on this point is Gerald J. Beyer, "Karl Rahner on the Radical Unity of the Love of God and Neighbour," *Irish Theological Quarterly* 68 (2003) 254–7.

33. "Reflections on the Unity of the Love of Neighbour and the Love of God," *TI* 6, 236; see *Love of Jesus and the Love of Neighbor* (New York: Crossroad, 1983); *Everyday Faith* (New York: Herder and Herder, 1968) 106–17. Rahner offered an existential and ontological interpretation of this unity: "The other, which mediates the person to itself, ever more clearly emerges as the personal other whom the person in knowledge and love encounters. The human environment is such only as a human and personal world in which man lives in order to come to himself, so that in love he abides with the other and thereby experiences what is meant by 'God' who is the sphere and the ultimate guarantee of interhuman love" (Rahner, "Foreword," Andrew Tallon, *Personal Becoming* [Milwaukee: University of Marquette Press, 1982] 3f.).

34. *F* 87.

35. "Reflections on the Unity . . . ," *TI* 6, 247f.

36. *J* 241.

37. G. Lohfink, "Universalismus und Exklusivität des Heils im Neuen Testament," in W. Kasper, ed., *Absolutheit des Christentums* (Freiburg: Herder, 1977) 66. For exegetes countering Hans Urs von Balthasar's view that a theology of grace outside of Christian externals has no support from the New Testament, see *SGW* 29–45.

38. *J* 241.

39. R. P. Meyer, *Universales Heil, Kirche und Mission. Karl Rahner und der Ephe-serbrief* (St. Augustin: Steyler, 1979) 213.

40. Rainer Kampling, "Exegese und Karl Rahner," in *TEG* 267–84.

41. See Heinz Kruse, "Die 'Anonymen Christen' exegetisch gesehen," *Münchener Theologische Zeitschrift* 18 (1967) 2–22.

42. See "The Christian among Unbelieving Relations," *TI* 3, 355–72.

43. *J* 241.

44. *R* 411.

45. Ibid. In the late sixteenth century, Domingo Bañez, commentator on Aqui-nas and adviser to Teresa of Avila, wrote: "It is sufficient that they be Christians in reality, for they have implicit faith. . . . Of course, that would not suffice for them to be called Christians" (*Commentaria in 2am 2ae* [Venice: Zilettum, 1586] col. 419); Aquinas anticipated modern theology when he wrote that grace is present in the intention, direction, orientation of the will "which with God is viewed as the deed" (*Summa Theologiae* III, 68, 2, 3). See John E. Perry, "Ripalda and Rahner. 400 Years of Jesuit Reflection on Universal Salvation," *Philosophy & Theology* 13:2 (2001) 339–61; and Rahner's forward to a study on Reginald Garrigou-Lagrange and this topic (Filipe José Couto, *Hoffnung im Unglauben. Zur Diskussion über den allgemeinen Heilswillen Gottes* [Paderborn: Schöningh, 1973]). See, too, Thomas O'Meara, "Tarzan, Las Casas and Rahner. Thomas Aquinas' Theology of Wider Grace," *Theology Digest* 45 (1998) 319–28 and—for Congar's view of Rahner's the-ology—O'Meara, "Yves Congar, Theologian of Grace in a Vast World," in Gabriel Flynn, ed., *Yves Congar* (Leuven: Peeters, 2005); John J. Pasquini, *Atheism and Salvation* (Lanham, MD: University Press of America, 2000).

46. *R* 411.

47. Ibid.

48. *R* 411f.

49. Doris Ziebritzki, *"Legitime Heilswege." Relecture der Religionstheologie Karl Rahners* (Innsbruck: Tyrolia, 2002) 54–9, 65f. The human spirit is essentially tran-scendence toward absolute Reality. The expression of this Mystery in concrete life, in knowing and free course of life, is what is called religion ("Theological Remarks on the Problem of Leisure," *TI* 4, 389).

50. Ziebritzki, *"Legitime Heilswege,"* 81.

51. Ibid., 31.

52. *F* 401.

53. *F* 164.

54. *F* 168. See Adolf Darlapp, "Der Weg der Heilsgeschichte," *MS* 1, 128–53.

55. *F* 164. Rahner's theology is too rich and analogous to be categorized as either "inclusivistic" or "exclusivistic" (Ziebritzki, *"Legitime Heilswege,"* 15, 185ff.); see "Jesus Christ in Non-Christian Religions," *F* 311–21.

Chapter 6

The Church
and Its Ministries

The church is changing. Change runs inexorably through the church's life, for people and institutions exist in time.

The church has changed considerably in the past fifty years. And yet, because the church changed so little in the second millennium of its history, each decade brings intimations of more change.

Contemporary life in the church unfolds as grace-in-history. A local church is a community, a collective person, a diocese or a parish, large or small, a place where grace comes to people. The church, local or worldwide, is not a business or a monarchy but a communion of people in service. In the church the reality and truth of God-in-Christ becomes not just present in ancient words and rites but in people living today; their faith and love find a community of support and actualization.[1] For Karl Rahner, the church is trinitarian and human. The Holy Spirit is a transcendental ground and source of Christian communal life, and the church is the sacrament, the incarnational reality furthering in men and women various ministries.

Is a church necessary? Do contemporary people find a church of superstition, of haughty control, attractive? Do not people leave the church not because of its teachings but because of boring performances and rigid structures? Essay after essay in *Theological Investigations* shows how the church could not just survive but flourish and serve. The church exists because men and women, families and groups, are social. Men and women need each other to express God's love and forgiveness. Jesus made gathering, community (what we call church), central to being his follower.

> A person cannot discover his personhood and his uniqueness by looking
> for them as something absolutely contrary to his social nature, but can
> only discover them within his social nature and in function of this social
> nature . . . because human persons are social beings, beings who can
> exist only within intercommunication with others. This pervades all the
> dimensions of human existence.[2]

Original sin is not the cause of the church nor is an arbitrary command
of Jesus. The social nature of humanity has been taken up into a special
plan and empowerment of God, "the kingdom of God."[3] Jesus' salvation
countering violence, sin, and ultimately death reaches all dimensions of
the human person. The church proceeds from Jesus' plan and intention,
becoming formed as the early communities meet the Jewish and Gentile
social worlds.

I. THE CHURCH AS EVENT AND COMMUNITY

The church is the people of God in a socially organized form and
a lasting historical presence. The world is not utterly secular nor is
Christianity about odd rituals. Bethlehem and Calvary show that God
can be present in social life. The church is not a better religion founded
by Jesus for a small group of the saved, but a community that is a sign, a
place where free subjectivity is touched by grace, and a history of God's
special plan is made concrete. For decades there has been a move out
of the narrow and insular imprisonment of grace, the locating of God's
presence in the soul or in the tabernacle situated in a gloomy church.

> Admittedly we have only weak and indistinct ideas of how a community
> formed by the new spirit of love of God and love of neighbor will appear
> in the concrete . . . , how it will express communal worship, being nei-
> ther a department store of holiness nor a cozy sect rejecting the world.
> The church understands its own reality best when it is actually fulfilling
> its function, actually speaking of God and his grace, of Jesus Christ and
> his Cross and Resurrection. . . . The church is still seeking to its goal
> through history. When it does that, the church appears not primarily as
> an institution acting upon us but as that which we all are through the
> reality of the grace of God moving, inspiring, and joining us together.[4]

The church is a place where God's will to save becomes visible. "The
church is the historical perdurance of Jesus Christ in a sacramental
concreteness within the life of grace of men and women . . . , a sacramental and social presence of the eschatological hope in and with
the Crucified and Risen Christ."[5] By forming the disciples, by stating
a lasting teaching, and by sending announcers of God's plan into the

entire world, Jesus founded a preaching and sacramental community. He founded the church in a general and global way so that it could unfold its forms through the centuries under the guidance of the Spirit.[6] The deepest insights of the Gospel are seminal realities capable of assuming varied forms—charism, ministry, sacramentality, forgiveness, life in the Spirit—for different churches in different places on earth. The church has its freedom to be the church, to be the church in the world.

Rahner wrote on a wide range of church topics: the episcopacy, the diaconate, the life of the priest, papal primacy, lay ministry, the church of sinners, theology of the priesthood, role of the papacy, limits of church authority and participation of all the baptized, and the potential falsehood of clericalism and of utopianism. He found in the church dedication and criticism, holiness and sin; he took for granted that the church is both the sacrament of Jesus' teaching and a socially constituted organization with limitations and history, with the value and the problematic of the ministries of bishops and the Roman pope.[7] Masterfully drawing church forms back to their sources, his theology gives a historico-cultural theology of the church and an existential ecclesiology for all the baptized. What does "people" in people of God mean? How does a charismatic grace assist a pope?

This ecclesiology unfolds in dialectic of global vision and local sensitivity. The church is not an idea or a principle, not a perfect society that nowhere exists, not a central administration, nor the product of church law.[8] Concreteness and local distinctness (aspects that central authority frequently fears and suppresses) make the church to be the church. Being a local church in Rahner's view, as William Clark observes, brings cultural and social elements and attitudes, art, and language, thus emphasizing that the church is a participant in human life.

> If the Spirit and its gifts are constitutive, then they must characterize all the loci of the church, so that the same Spirit that is understood to guarantee the work of the hierarchy is also acknowledged at work directly within the local community, then it is necessarily at work in all the contextual elements and human relationships that constitute that community and its setting.[9]

The entire church is in the local church, and vice versa.

As was mentioned, Rahner was an important figure at Vatican II. An early address about the coming council chose the line from Paul's First Letter to the Thessalonians, "Do not extinguish the Spirit." Moving in a few months from being a theologian censored by the Vatican to serving as a valued contributor, he was active in drafting the conciliar texts on revelation and the church. In the meeting rooms within the Vatican, a stream of ideas was assisted by his competent, even elegant Latin. Somewhere I acquired mimeographed pages of Rahner's observations on the schema *De Ecclesia in mundo huius temporis* (The Church in the Modern World) in the draft of May 26, 1965, written at Munich during the spring before the last session of the council. His comments were divided into general and specific (he observed that the Latin style needed extensive improvement!). "This schema constructed, despite many difficulties, by so many different people working so intensely in different areas is still deficient in many ways." How is the contemporary person to think about Christian revelation guiding the church in the wider world? Statements, although they do leave behind prior neo-Scholastic terminology, are vague, and an engaging manner of expression is missing from a text too abstract, one possibly too optimistic. Should there not be added a Christian anthropology, including a theology of sin and one of the future? Yves Congar recalled Rahner at the council: "Rahner spoke a great deal but always had something to say (perhaps that was an indiscretion). When Rahner spoke it was with heart and soul."[10]

Letters to friends during and after the council described the fatiguing and meticulous course of conciliar work. The end of the council in December 1965 was marked in Munich, Germany, by a special lecture delivered by Rahner in the Herkulessaal, an auditorium in the former residence of the Bavarian royalty used for symphony concerts. He spoke of the council's goals, of its entry into history, of its service of faith, hope, and love among the human family. The church obligates itself to pursue what the documents say (otherwise the deliberations are a deceptive theater).

> The Second Vatican Council is the first council of a World Church that really wants to be a World Church and not a Church with European exports to all parts of the world. . . . Was renewal bestowed by the Council? No, but the event was a decisive beginning: the church cannot go backwards to the age before it.[11]

Conciliar measures will not find fulfillment in ten years, for it took the Council of Trent a hundred years until it had sustained results. Still, a new theology of the church, a new emphasis on the local church, have arrived. The underlying constitution of the church is the Holy Spirit leading communities to be a serving sacrament for the world and not a bureaucracy of power. "From now on, the Catholic will think and experience the church as the 'vanguard,' the sacramental sign, the manifestation in history of a grace of salvation which takes effect far beyond the confines of the visible church as sociologically definable."[12]

Karl Lehmann, Albert Raffelt, and others hold that Rahner's later writings after 1970 display a new ecclesial tonality.[13] The people of God are a community in history in service to and in dialogue with the world. For Michael Fahey,

> Rahner's ecclesiology in the late 60's and 70's is descriptive and phenomenological. Again it is characterized by probing analyses of solutions and crises. In one sense it is less interdogmatic or systematic than it was at an earlier stage, where Rahner was anxious to show more explicitly the interconnectedness of church and grace, church and Trinity, or church and sacraments.[14]

The following pages will look at the forms of the church, at ministries formed by charism, and at leadership and authority.

II. THE CHURCH EXISTING IN HISTORY'S FORMS

To address people in cultures and ages, the church lives out of tradition and proclamation. A seminal depth of message seeks new expressions. In the church, the transcendental dynamic of grace tends to the concrete to serve the community through history. Jesus had given the human family not a list of rites, pious propositions, and church offices, but basic realities capable of appearing in diverse forms in new realizations. Sacrament is an analogical reality: there are different levels and kinds of realities capable of holding grace. Jesus, the Word as a human being, is the sacrament and the source of all sacramental union of grace and creation. The church is not mainly an institution, but the Body of Christ, incarnational like its Head.

> The church is nothing else than the further projection of the reality of Jesus through space and time. Every word of the church's message, every sacramental sign is a part of the world in its earthiness with which the Spirit has united itself indissolubly since the day on which the Logos became flesh.[15]

The incarnational is the sacramental.

The personal influence of grace in people fashions churches. In Rahner's ecclesiology,

> there is an arch from a personal point of departure to the content of his theology of ministry, a dynamic moving from the self-communication of God as grace to the person. . . . Rahner's theology of church and ministry fashions a bridge between transcendence and concreteness. The church is an open system, charismatic, having a potential to change through the grace effective in each member. Questions of structure and issues of the unfolding and ordering of ministry remain open and flexible.[16]

The church is the fundamental, living sacrament of ways of God's Spirit touching people.

> We have called the church the fundamental sacrament not by a vague borrowing of the concept of sacrament known to us from current texts on the seven sacraments but by deriving the idea of sacrament from Christology. Fundamental sacrament means for us the one abiding symbolic presence (similar in structure to the Incarnation) of the eschatological redemptive grace of Christ.[17]

Sacrament means more than the seven sacraments, more than the approach a century ago when sacraments were isolated encounters of God with an individual: sacraments and sacramentals are the material realizations of the Holy Spirit (of grace and charism) in the world.

> Wherever and however the church is this ultimate sacrament of salvation for the world there Christ is present in his Spirit and there he makes his presence tangible, even though it may be in a way that is "anonymous." Because of this the Lord himself says that he is present, though unrecognized, wherever one person shows compassion from his heart to another.[18]

Bread and wine are not abstract: they relate to the life of the recipient; the words of the readings are not general. The event of a sacrament occurs in a world where there is grace, in a life already graced: the mediation of material things and words and people focus grace into human life. Puritanism is the enemy, not the friend of religion and grace, for it pushes away the very means, for most humans, of making grace convincing and attractive. Circles of central sacraments move out from their center, Jesus, through the life of the church, and then sacramental flowers and palms and water also spring up from the foundational sacrament of the church and its Head. The Spirit takes seriously social existentials, as the history of the church shows that liturgical and ministerial forms may come in cultural variety. Catholics live in a church where sacramentals extend the sacraments outward. What is celebrated is not something esoteric or theatrical, not magical productions of God's grace. What is occurring in life is explicitly described and made significant and visible in special moments in the church. "Even dogmatically permanent and divinely ordained structures in the Church have always had a historically conditioned concrete form."[19] Sacraments come forth from the life cycle of a person or the festivals of a society.

> The individual sacraments are concrete acts of self-fulfillment on the part of the church as the primary sacramental of the liturgy of the world.

Worship activities designate the same grace that the basic sacrament of
the church designates: that grace that is present and effective within the
world constantly. They are not extrinsic processes touching upon an un-
hallowed world from without but manifestations of the grace operative
in the world.[20]

Salvation is liturgy in life. Harvey Egan sees the sacraments as "epipha-
nanizations," celebrations and realizations of grace in everyday life.[21]
They signify emotionally and intellectually what is occurring in human
lives all the time.

Sacramental rites can become a static system or a superstition, injurious to people, and so the Spirit is always at work to renew teaching
and liturgy. Here, too, the distinction between a transcendental gift of
grace and categorical knowledge and action is basic. Grace in a transcendental mode, "the kingdom of God," gives life to the categorical rites
and vestments, the texts and books of the church past and present. The
transcendental is the source (and the critic) of categorical church forms.
The divine transcendental has a global richness open to styles and forms
in a history of realizations; the Communion cup, the window of light, a
crucifix holding a different style from the fifth, thirteenth, and seventeenth centuries. In the decades after the council, as renewal opened up
rigid medieval and Baroque forms, Rahner treated in countless talks and
essays the history of the ideas and forms of the Christian community.
Vatican II showed an emptiness in the church's life and sought to renew
sacrament and ministry. What is perduring and what is changeable, what
comes from Jesus and his Spirit, and what is unhealthy and quite transitory? Ecclesiology and ecclesial life exist today in a movement of change,
change from lines in an old textbook and legal institutions to the vital
life of a local church. "The concrete forms of the church show the church
pointing beyond itself to a richer realization of what it is called to be."[22]
History always moves forward, and the church may not find life solely in
the past; no basic return to the past is possible, and the avoidance of the
future is injurious. The church is the continuance of the event of Christ
and the sacrament of eschatological victory.

Today's issues—historically diversified ministries from primal ministry, central authority and local church, ephemeral devotions and
virtual sacramentalities, Christ in a history of religions amid a world of
grace—are concrete even as they refer to what is most basic: the Holy
Spirit and the community in history.[23]

Human beings live in many worlds with their own public liturgies
of the human and the divine, and the Christian community mediates
between liturgies. Michael Skelley wrote an essay on Rahner's theology

as a liturgy of the world. "The liturgy of the world is simultaneously a human achievement and a gift of God."[24] While the liturgy of the church is radically caused and sustained by God, it is also something we accomplish. We are not called to be passive spectators at the church's worship, but to enter, freely and fully, into it. God's presence in history with its climax in the drama of Jesus Christ is the liturgy of the world, and the church's rituals and words and ministers exist to empower and interpret grace in the world, "not as divine liturgy in the world but as the divine liturgy of the world, as manifestation of the divine liturgy which is identical with salvation history."[25]

Rahner's theology of worship interprets the church's liturgy for people who are tempted to dismiss it as irrelevant and superstitious.

> The Mass-goer need not be alarmed and feel that his faith is in danger if he is tempted to see the sacraments as empty ceremonies . . . he need not imagine that when they are performed God does something he would not do if they were omitted. Rather he must realize that they spring from, express, and lead to the divine depths of real life. . . . Everyone has such experiences, and it is the duty of theological instruction not to produce them but to bring them into reflex awareness. The Mass is only a small sign of the Mass of the world.[26]

Sunday worship highlights the experiences of God in ordinary life. There are not two forms of relating to God, personal prayer and parish Mass, but several ways. Surrounded and born by God's grace, believers turn to God in ways of prayer, circles of the sacramental, moments caught in the lights of candles or in the eyes of people. Liturgy can join beautiful singing to architecture of stone and glass, or it may lead out to the needs of children or the desperation of the homeless.

> The Eucharistic liturgy that is celebrated in church must break out of its self-centeredness and self-preoccupation to give ritual expression to the liturgy of the world that it exists to serve. All of this means further that broadening the notion of liturgy and of sacramentality by seeing them primarily in the context of the reign of God rather than of the church.[27]

The worship of the church is important and significant not because something happens in it that does not happen elsewhere, but because it makes present and explicit in sacrament and liturgy what lies less perceived in the world.

III. CHARISM AND MINISTRY AND OFFICE

The people of God live out the Trinity's self-communication becoming visible in ritual and active in service.

Did Jesus found the church's offices and rites? He founded disciples in a community with sacramentality and ministry—but in a global, seminal way. Not listing rites and offices, Jesus set in motion a dynamic force capable of drawing from times and cultures various forms. Ministry like sacramentality is given by Jesus to the church in a largely transcendental mode, and the New Testament records its incipient concrete forms (disciples, apostles, elders, deacons). Church documents of the first centuries list a number of ministries; later there is an expansion of ministry and also a contraction. The bishop, the presbyter, and the deacon have their own histories through the centuries. Jesus gave a basic ministerial reality to the church by Jesus and his Spirit, and this unfolds into various ministries (a view in contrast to the nineteenth-century perspective that Jesus founded the papacy and episcopacy, and they founded other major and minor orders).[28]

The baptism of Christians is not an initiation into a closed sect, a certificate of membership for a next life, or a private moment of individual salvation, but an entry into the life and mission of the church: the Spirit is preparing personal and new charisms of ministry for the baptized, and there is no lack of people ready and willing to respond. Church ministry is "based on the laity as personal believers, and less on the institutional element and its power in society or on the clergy as the traditional supports and recipients of its social prestige."[29] Already in the 1950s, Rahner had written an essay on "the lay apostolate": that term drew together a loose assembly of devotional practices and church enterprises from the first half of the twentieth century seeking ways for laity to serve the church in an "apostolate." "Lay" is not profane, for a layperson cannot be someone outside the circle of the Spirit. Each baptized Christian has a role in the church, and so the church can no longer be an institution of clergy and passive laity in that rigid, divisive social format that had lasted for a millennium.[30] Catholic Action proved to be not enough, for most of the laity remained passive: Catholic men and women held a potentiality awaiting liberation. The church is an open system, a kind of community whose condition cannot fully be determined from one legal text or office.

A book from 1958, *The Dynamic Element in the Church,* developed the theme of charism. Far from containing only an occasional mystical charismatic like Vincent de Paul or the Little Flower in the church, the charismatic comes to all the baptized. Theology portraying grace in a personal mode leads to grace as the dynamic of the community. Charisms are not rare, miraculous displays but grace, *"charis,"* at work in all the baptized. The Spirit offers more than an elite priesthood and passive laity, and the texts of Vatican II gave an impetus to see the baptized as active in the church, to free grace to serve the community and society. The church's institutions at any one time have limits, but the Spirit does not. "When Christians as such act, the church acts in them. Their action is an activity of the church, not because it is wholly organized by the church's hierarchy but because it is inspired and guided by the Spirit of the church."[31]

Rahner had a hope and a vision for the church where a healthier sacramentality and a variety of church ministry would emerge around the world. "When the bearers of hierarchical jurisdiction are seen as such *because there is church,* because there are those who make up the church, then certainly a one-sided view of the church as an authoritarian institution of salvation is overcome. The church appears then as *those who we all are.*"[32] The living realization of the charismatic in all Christians—a first and most proper characteristic of the church—begins with "the Lord of the church presiding over the church as open system."[33] The Spirit is pressing the church to give practical effect to this new awareness of the activity of all, while the ecclesial source of the new vitality is baptism. Baptismal grace gives the right, the task, and the interior power to help the church realize itself today. The church listens to divine revelation and hears the needs of an age in the same moment. The cultural and religious situation helps the reception of the Gospel realize, incarnate itself in a new way.[34]

> Each member of the church is an active co-bearer of the self-construction of the church, and precisely as this self-construction of the church means concretely the mediation of salvation to the individual. But this fact does not mean that the function through which the individual Christian is co-bearer of the self-construction of the church is the same for all individuals.[35]

The theologian viewed positively an expanding number of ministers, a diversity of ministries, and expected for some an appropriate liturgy of commissioning. As the church became less clerical and hierarchical, a wider responsibility for the church displayed the sacramental nature of the church. Michael Fahey sums up: "Rahner had an acute sense of personal freedom and the importance of the individual in the church. The individual Christian was never considered in isolation but in her or his ecclesial context. Piety was ecclesial piety."[36]

The sacramentality of the church is visible in a group of ministries expanding out of the basic reality of the church.

IV. A TRANSCENDENTAL COMMUNITY OF MINISTERS

A theology of the church as a transcendental reality with a richness of forms in the community offered a theology of variety for church life. The Catholic Church must question its present situation where unnecessary requirements limit those who might enter the three ordained ministries. The church's mission and origin imply that its ministries are different from those of secular officeholders. "Office has a functional character in the church as a society, even though this society with its functions (proclamation of the word, sacrament, leadership of the church's life as society) constitutes a sign of the reality of the church—the free Spirit, faith, hope and love."[37] Church leadership needs to respect the dignity and freedom of all Christians and humbly coordinate what Jesus and his Spirit have bestowed.

> Christians are the church and should not merely be regarded as the subject of her directives and the object of her solicitude and protection. . . . By sacramental consecration every Christian in the church has been authorized and empowered for the task of actively co-operating in the work of the church both interiorly and exteriorly.[38]

Rahner welcomed the restoration of ancient ministries and the establishment of new ministries. A point of departure for understanding the development of ministries was seeing—as with the diaconate—how these ministries already existed, ministries in education, social services, and liturgy. At Vatican II he called attention to the fact that aspects of the diaconate were being done by men at that time but without ordination or participation in the liturgy.[39] Rahner often referred to the reality of ministry, noting that the baptized were doing ministry habitually and professionally without having received any sacramental commissioning, which commissioning existed in the church precisely to assist them in ministry, giving reference to "a sacramental and therefore pneumatic basis for the transmission of every ministerial office . . . , a law rooted in the Pneuma itself."[40] Should not office and ordination further confirm that reality? Why should they stay back in the shadows of ecclesiastical offices, isolated from a sacramental confirmation in grace? The church exists in a wider ministerial form than bishops and priests, and so new and old ministries exist not as an "apostolate" (a slight extension of the pastor and bishop) but as ecclesial ministries. The parish services of the baptized are in fact offices in the church even if the church has not given partial or full recognition to those ministries.

Today the baptized are leaders of parishes. A theology of grace leads the Christian faithful to the source of ministry, while the charismatic dimension becomes objectified in a wider ministry for the church around the world. Ulrich Möbs writes:

> In contrast to John Paul II's *Christfideles laici,* it is not the sacramental ordination which is the presupposition and beginning for the one with an office and a ministry but the work and goal of the ministry, the content of the function. The Christian who without ordination is fulfilling an official ministry in the church can be an "anonymous" minister and officeholder under certain conditions. . . . Ordination is normally and fully constitutive for the office but there can be "anonymous" offices (ministries) without an explicit ordination but where there has been an implicit designation.[41]

Should not office and ordination further confirm that reality? Even if the church does not give a ministry a title or an ordination ceremony, it may still exist.

The center of church life is preaching the Word and offering the Eucharist. The priests and deacons form a college around the bishop who is the leader of the local church. The diocese, the local church, is a unity and all its members are servants of the being and activity of the church. The priest, for Rahner, is "based in a community and commissioned by the church to be the full and official preacher of the Word of God so that the sacramentally highest level of intensity of this word is entrusted to him."[42] The priest as celebrant of liturgy does not exhaust his identity but is a part of a wider ministry involving preaching and leadership. The pastor is not the sole recipient of divine empowerment. If the priest-pastor is at the center of the life of the church, still that ministry does not exhaust all ministry. The essence of the priesthood is not simply to confect the Eucharist, but to be a pastor, a leader

> in all the dimensions of church life, including the Eucharist as the culmination of the sacramental word in the church. In the church before Vatican II there was really only one ministry, and now, there are others. Every believer is called to ministry. That the church has chosen at times in history a pattern of three ordained ministries is important and yet does not preclude that variations and additions can come.[43]

Various roles of leadership, of service to the word and Spirit, although not joined to a particular sacrament, now are active in leadership and service. "Office is never simply identical with the Spirit and can never replace the Spirit; office is really credible and effective in the sight of people only when the presence of the Spirit is evident and not merely when formal mission and authority are involved, however legitimate these may be."[44] Why reduce ecclesiology to a contrast of aspects of lay and nonordained ministers? It is better to fashion ways of "conferring of an office of a permanent character . . . regarded as sacramental."[45] Can there be in the church beyond bishop, priest, and deacon, other functions in the church that are the same or analogous to the three levels of *Ordo*?

> The ecclesial reality [past and present] of the church proves that outside the three offices there are other ministries in the church which ultimately are not simply ways of assisting the priesthood in a secular way but which partake at least in an analogous way in the mission and task of the sacral ministry of the church.[46]

Religious educators, liturgists, and others working in social services are such. Could they not take part in ministry and sacramentality as the three ordained offices do? The church, distinguishing between "one pastoral ministry" and its "degrees," is interested not in quantitative control but in fullness and quality.[47]

> Rahner finds a great urgency in recognizing and affirming the sacramental dimension of the significant and important ministerial tasks that are carried out by non-ordained members of the church. . . . Those who share in the church's one ministerial office in significant ways must have that participation confirmed as to its full meaning. Not to do so is to diminish the church itself as the basic sacrament.[48]

Rahner's writings were published when what became lay ecclesial ministry with its diverse forms in Germany, the United States and Canada, in Central and Latin America, was beginning. In the 1970s, as the German church instituted ministries of pastoral assistants in a parish, he observed the introduction of full-time ministries into a parish team, and the leadership of the nonordained in directing parishes for which priests were not available. Those new theological issues and consequences appeared within an ecclesiology of ministry as a transcendental reality.

Themes of the people of God, baptismal ministries, and a dignity of individuals lead to the issue of women in the church. Already in 1964 Rahner had addressed the new situation of women in the ministry and was directing a dissertation on their ordination.[49] Again the theology of de facto ministry was helpful. Ordination to diaconate, episcopacy, or presbyterate, is the entrance to canonically approved office, but there are now other accesses to full-time ministries for professionally educated men and women. Women in numbers are in the ministry, acting as assistant pastors and then as pastors. Rahner put things in a startling way:

> Where the church, with or without ordination, not just for an individual case but habitually, professionally and officially hands to someone an aspect of this power which distinguishes the clergy from laity it makes that person into a cleric quite apart from whether they are so called or not. In this strict theological sense a woman can indeed belong to the clergy . . . [50]

In 1977 he addressed the Vatican's discouraging declaration on women by noting that, although such a text should receive respect, it also needs critique. First, it gives few arguments to support its generally negative position, for the document simply argues other positions down. Second, the document does not look at the pastoral practice of the church today and it does not offer a clear theology of what it means by priesthood. Third, the basic Vatican argument is that Jesus and apostles did not ordain women; this argument ignores the cultural-historical situation; the structure of Judaism and of the Christian communities would have been influential as Jewish religion or the culture of the Mediterranean worlds in the first century conditioned Jesus and the apostles.

> In the cultural and social situation of their time Jesus and the early church could not conceive of, much less introduce, women to be leaders of the community and Eucharist. . . . They did not notice the contradiction between their generally high position of the woman (which distanced itself from the understanding of that time) and their concrete praxis. . . .[51]

An ecclesiology for women depends upon a view of history, upon ways in which cultural forms express the Spirit, upon the metamorphoses of sacramentality and ministry, upon distinguishing between human traditions and divine realities. "When the Congregation for the Faith declares that it is impossible to admit women to the priesthood, then I have to argue against it and affirm from a dogmatic point of view that the priesthood of women is not impossible."[52]

Lay ecclesial ministry as reality and diversity can still find today some basic principles in Rahner's ecclesiology of transcendental fullness and historical forms.

V. LEADERS IN THE CHURCH

The bishop is the head of the local church and not just the representative of one particular bishop, the Bishop of Rome. The bishop's ministry comes from the Spirit of Jesus, and the role of the pope is one

of organizational appointment. Titular bishops, auxiliary bishops, and
cardinals should not encroach upon the ministry of the bishop, and the
independence of the bishops is not a residue from a time before Char-
lemagne, but a facet of the church as real as the role of the Bishop of
Rome.[53] In the church, bishops receive a "promised support of the Spirit
of Christ," "a specific charism."[54]

The bishop's ministry should be rooted in the local church, in consultation and representation, and not be separate from the charisms and
ministries of the baptized.

> The doctrinal authority attached to the teaching office is a derivation
> from the church as a whole (and in itself and not merely in respect to
> the content of what is proclaimed), or in virtue of the fact that those who
> proclaim it are always first and foremost themselves believers involved in
> the history of faith in the church as a whole. . . . This derivation from
> the *church* is precisely the concrete form in which the derivation of the
> teaching office from Christ and God is realized. . . . In terms of this
> faith, this history of faith, this development of dogma—the magisterium
> is concretely dependent on these—all the members of the church are
> active, each in its own way, through life, confession of faith, prayer, con-
> crete decisions, or pondered theology: and all these ways are not simply
> the execution of the truths and norms coming from the magisterium.[55]

Tradition sees the bishop as important because he represents his local
church and its faithful members.

> [There is in Vatican II] a clear rejection of the idea implicit in the prac-
> tice of recent years that a bishop is nothing more than a subordinate of-
> ficial of the pope. The bishop directs his flock by his own (not delegated)
> ordinary power in the name of Christ and not in the name of the pope.
> To the bishop is fully committed the pastoral office in its normal form
> and cannot therefore consider himself to be a mere recipient and execu-
> tor of commands received from higher quarters, a mere executive organ
> of universal ecclesiastical laws or of initiatives emanating from Rome."[56]

In the decades after Vatican II, the structure and ethos of authority in
the church is moving in new directions. One office, the Petrine ministry
in Rome, had, through developments in the eleventh, seventeenth, and
twentieth centuries, come to dominate all others. Powerful popes in the
half centuries on either side of 1900 bore the name Pius, and a Roman
centrism defined the "Pian epoch."[57] Already in 1964, Rahner observed
that the pope is not what is ordinarily understood by a monarch: the office is not hereditary and lasts for a few years. The papacy is itself bound
to church structures, to the gospel, to the will of the Holy Spirit, and to

the bishops; it should be balanced by the charismatic variety of the entire church. The holders of the Petrine office should not seek dominance but should accept limitations to their jurisdiction, pursuing consultation and freely developing structures for facing new issues.

> The future presses in upon the church, a future in which the premium set upon the characteristics present in the local church . . . will perhaps be higher even than it is in the present. . . . Life in the church in the new form which it will acquire in the future will first, and by anticipation be experienced here in the local church.[58]

As Vatican II gave prominence to the identity of a bishop and to the role of the bishops as a college, the pendulum that had for four hundred years moved toward the papacy began to move back toward bishops and other Christians.

> Catholic ecclesiology of former times from the period of the Reformation onwards was concerned almost exclusively with the institutional factors in the church. It viewed the church as a *'societas perfecta,'* unified, organized, and directed by the official hierarchy which is in its turn summed up in a supreme and effective manner in the pope. . . . Meanwhile the interior subjective holiness achieved by justifying grace was regarded as existing almost exclusively as grace in the individual's solitary existence.[59]

The pope as leader of the bishops around the world and as European bishop or patriarch are two different ministries.

The bishops are in search of their full identity, of their roles in preaching and theologizing; they are not above but within the church, and along with all the baptized and ministers ponder how grace through charism becomes in an individual a distinctive ministry. A bishop, expected to be more than an aloof bank president, should have the qualities of a leader, a leader in public preaching and in serving what the Spirit wants for this local church. The bishop should be the gift of a sacrament, not the survivor of a political intrigue and administrative mandate; he leads his people not as a delegate of the pope, but from the Spirit of Christ. "The bearer of the highest and fullest power in the church is the college of bishops with the pope at its head."[60] Present pastoral needs require the bishop to be a preacher of some ability and an animator of ministries, to be visible and articulate in large urban settings.

The collegiality of the bishops in their regional conferences calls for a papacy relating to the bishops in mature ways. There should be episcopal representatives of the bishop conferences, chosen by these conferences, who meet in Rome at regular intervals and who constitute an advisory body to the pope. It would have priority over the Vatican administrators and be immediately attached to the pope as responsible for legislation in the church. Those bishops chosen by their regional church would elect the pope and direct the church when the pope became incapacitated.[61] The papacy is within the church, not above it.

> That prophets [from the distant past] are praised and canonized is fine—then they are dead and their charism can be institutionally accepted. More important is the discernment of charisms of the Spirit when they emerge; the furthering of charisms and the avoidance of letting them suffocate from misunderstanding and neglect, even from hatred and mean-spiritedness. That is not so easy, for while the institution is always the same . . . , the charismatic is essentially new and surprising.[62]

It is dangerous for the church to marginalize the people of God, to stifle the gifts of the Spirit. "Obviously the entire ecclesiastical apparatus, from the pope and all the Roman offices to all the bishops and churches, from sacraments to monetary contributions exists for only one purpose: to arouse in people a little bit of faith, hope and love."[63]

The teaching authority of the pope and bishops does not give new revelation from God but mediates and serves the faith of the church in Jesus Christ.

> This teaching authority simply interprets, develops and actualizes in ever new historical concrete situations the message of Christ. . . . It is the concrete organ and the embodiment of the historical tangibility of the whole church's understanding of the faith, and this understanding is ultimately mediated to it by the Spirit of Jesus Christ and through the victory of his grace.[64]

Much remains to be said about the participation of all the church in the formation of teaching authority and its relationship to education and conscientious Catholics.

The teaching authority of the church will need to move from repeating antique or abstract phrases to a true teaching in which people hear their faith. "The believing, 'hearing' church is not simply the audience to which authority condescends."[65] History brings a compendium of truth needing further insight and application. Christianity is "not a castle of truth with innumerable rooms which must be occupied in order to be 'in the truth' but is the opening from which all individual truths (even errors) lead into the Truth which is the inconceivability of God."[66] Change in the church does include earlier views, and the church has a memory, although tradition, more than memory, is the life of the church expressing the Gospel for today. The magisterium of the church must admit its own existentials—its cultural background, its education, its pastoral experience, its limitations, its prejudices—and accept the universal paradigm of God's sovereign self-presence in a limited, sinful individual.[67]

His specific theology of ministry—from lector to pope—is an aspect of the theology of the church. Ulrich Möbs writes: "His dogmatic theology of ministry, far from being static and intolerant, pursues new ways . . . , a theology drawn from many small studies on church office written over forty years."[68] The church is endowed with divine gifts, yet employs those gifts through human activities. It has not locked up the truths of Truth but seeks to respond to the divine Spirit teaching in subtle ways the truth.

VI. THE CHURCH TODAY

Rahner, Jesuit and theologian, remained a man of the church; the firmness of his faith consciously tempered by his historical appreciation of the church led him to be critical of the church when it embraced deformity, avoided history, and served its own power. Even more, it led Rahner to imagine a renewal of the forms of church life and the creation of new liturgical and institutional structures.

> The one church of the future will not be the Roman Catholic Church in the form that it exists today. It will be marked by a legitimate pluralism, a much greater pluralism than that which has existed in Roman Catholicism. . . . The church will be made up of a network of small basic communities with some kind of organized inter-relationship. This commonality will be assured by the bishops. There will have to be a pope, but much else will be different. Present Roman centralism will no longer exist. It will not be allowed to exist. This opinion is quite compatible with the conviction that Rome will, from many points of view, have a greater significance throughout the world than it does today.[69]

Rahner saw early on two new contexts for ecclesial life. First, there were cultures and languages of peoples newly Christian that would offer new forms of being-the-community. Second, he saw that education and the media would require an openness in discussing issues. The opinions of Catholics reported by the media about ethical issues or maturity in church leadership amid differing theological perspectives would be inescapable once the views of so many were publicly known, views gathered from around the world.

> We must get used to such disagreements within the church. We must learn that the unity of the faith and the intention to obedience and love

are not abolished by certain tensions. Both sides must get used to this: the authorities must not imagine that peace and quiet are the foremost necessity, and the laity must not think that revolution and rebellion against authority and arbitrary theological opinions are ideal attitudes.[70]

If he was critical of Hans Küng's setting aside of papal infallibility, he also publicly disagreed with decisions of the Vatican: the rejection of J. B. Metz for a university position in Munich, procedures against Edward Schillebeeckx and Gustavo Gutierrez, and the Vatican's attempts to control the Society of Jesus. He was an early and perceptive critic of the new direction around 1980 to block the dynamics of Vatican II. "The ecclesial critique of Karl Rahner is embraced by a 'Yes' always greater than the church, by a love struggling for more breadth and fluid variety in the church."[71] Renewal and change are normal for a living church.

> In the church there will always be conservative and progressive trends, both of which in principle are necessary and useful when change needs to be combined with continuity. . . . The struggle about earthly things in the church is often carried on with a passion usually devoted to the eternal. But if the distinction is seen and made clear in regard to controversies on true or false structural changes in the church it could help to defuse the struggles up to a point.[72]

He stressed the possibility of reexpressing doctrines and the freedom of conscience of Christians.

What of the church of today? In his last fifteen years, Rahner addressed dozens of concrete issues in the church, showing how change could be positive and revelatory of the impetus given by the Spirit. He described the church of the future as declericalized and noted the various ways in which the church was not a totalitarian monarchy but a limited democracy. Walter Schmolly sees Rahner summing up and passing beyond his times.

> For the twentieth century Rahner created—he is certainly the only theologian of whom one can say this—an ecclesiology of the century. He succeeded in drawing the 1930s and the period of upheaval after World War I into his fashioning of a convincing self-understanding of the church drawing on the great theological traditions and dogmatic expressions of the past so that in the form of a continuous, ever deepening movement of theology this ecclesiology could accompany the church through the century as it met the process of modernity and reached a highpoint at Vatican II.[73]

The time after the council offers great hope because it offers to the church around the world opportunities for life, for growth beyond being an idol, being only a bureaucracy.

Every subtle theology, every dogma, every church law, every accommodation and denial of the church, every institution, every bureau and all its powers, every holy liturgy and every mission has as its only goal: faith, hope and love towards God and man. All other plans and deeds of the church would be absurd and perverse were she to abandon this commission and seek only the church's self.[74]

A Rahnerian theology of degrees of implicit and explicit grace has an important role to play in church life, explaining the expansion of the ministry since Vatican II, the variety of ministries in different countries, the new model of parish team led by the pastor, ministries in universities and cities, in rural areas, and in institutions of health care. As Christian ministry needs a transcendental analysis of the local church, a broader theology of the Spirit, a pneumatology of the world, affirms the gift of grace as given to all.

Does Rahner's view of wider grace touching each person diminish mission into the world? To the contrary, Karl Lehmann finds there a missionary dynamic and a marked characteristic of service.[75] Ministry and mission in today's world require attentive theological consideration. If human cultures and religions flow to and from the event of Jesus Christ, and if the church is more than an agent of European colonialism, the responding theology is not solely the conversion of blocks of populations, but a setting forth of a psychology and sociology of how people in various ways respond to grace. His theology points to the reality that mission and inculturation are facets of wider grace; grace lies implicit in the forms waiting to be drawn by the Christian church to its explicit forms. The mission of the church is to make explicit what is implicit: that has been the mission of the Word in Jesus. Mission is not a universal theory but a local dynamic, drawing people to the local church. The church's mission exists not to divide or condemn humanity but to draw forth what is most human.

> The Christian's zeal has the greatest chance of success when enthusiasm for missionary vocation is tempered by calmness and patience, the patience of God (which, according to Paul is positively salvific rather than condemnatory in its meaning) . . . God does not begin the work of his grace only at that stage at which someone takes it up in the name of God.[76]

Christians meet others as brothers and sisters who need to be drawn to an awareness of the grace that lies within them. Christian mission and ministry announces the explicit dawn of the reign of God, the great events centered in Jesus, and God's plan for the future of humanity moving away from error and superstition caused by religious things.[77] A church of diversity, of cultural sacramentalization, open to its primal diversity and participation and moving away from clericalism and sectarianism, a church open to people and honest in its representation of the Gospel—this church lies ahead.

> Everything of the church, therefore everything institutional, legal, sacramental, every word, every occupation in the church and therefore every reform of all these ecclesiastical realities, is in the last analysis . . . something simple and yet so difficult and blessed at the same time: faith, hope, and love in the hearts of all people.[78]

This theology of history and the future leads us to the next chapter.

NOTES

1. *HPT* 1, 124; Walter Schmolly surveys the studies on Rahner's ecclesiology and gives a history of its development from early articles to postconciliar essays in *Eschatologische Hoffnung in Geschichte. Karl Rahners dogmatisches Grundverständnis der Kirche als theologische Begleitung von deren Selbstvollzug* (Innsbruck: Tyrolia, 2001) and "Karl Rahners systematischer Verstehensansatz der Kirche," in R. Siebenrock, *Karl Rahner in der Diskussion* (Innsbruck: Tyrolia, 2001) 269–88; see Fu-Long Lien, *Die Ekklesiologie in der Theologie Karl Rahner* (Ammersbek: Jensen, 1990); Marek Chojnacki, *Die Nähe des Unbegreifbaren. Der moderne philosophische Kontext der Theologie Karl Rahners und seine Konsequenzen in dieser Theologie* (Fribourg: Universitätsverlag, 1996) 321–44; Heinz Schuster, "Karl Rahners Ansatz einer existentialen Ekklesiologie," *WT* 370–86, and works cited in this chapter.

2. *F* 323, 412.

3. *SGG* 133–4; see Michael Fahey, "On Being Christian—Together," in Leo O'Donovan, ed., *A World of Grace* (New York: Seabury, 1980) 120–37; Francis Schüssler Fiorenza, *Foundational Theology: Jesus and the Church* (New York: Crossroad, 1984) 91–5.

4. "The New Image of the Church," *TI* 10, 4, 5, 26f.; "Church of Non-simultaneity," *The Shape of the Church to Come* (New York: Seabury, 1974) 35f.

5. Schmolly, *Eschatologische Hoffnung in Geschichte*, 256, 258.

6. *F* 335.

7. See various interviews in *KRD*.

8. The church should avoid "ecclesiological monophysitism" where the church hides behind an idealized description of the church found only in past textbooks of apologetics ("On the Structure of the People in the Church Today," *TI* 12, 218f.).

9. Clark, "The Authority of Local Church Communities: Perspectives from the Ecclesiology of Karl Rahner," *Philosophy & Theology* 13 (2001) 423.

10. Yves Congar, "Erinnerungen an Karl Rahner auf dem Zweiten Vatikanum," in *Karl Rahner. Bilder eines Lebens* (Freiburg: Herder, 1985) 67; see H. Vorgrimler, "Karl Rahner: The Theologian's Contribution," in A. Stacpoole, ed., *Vatican II Revisited* (Minneapolis: Winston, 1986); Colleen Frances O'Reilly, "The Emergence

of a World Church: Karl Rahner's Theological Interpretation of the Second Vatican Council" (Ph.D. dissertation, St. Michael's College, Toronto, n.d.); Franz Kardinal König, "Erinnerungen an Karl Rahner als Konzilstheologen," in A. Raffelt, *Karl Rahner in Erinnerung* (Düsseldorf: Patmos, 1994) 149–61.

11. "The New Image of the Church," *TI* 10, 14.

12. Ibid.

13. Lehmann, Raffelt, "Einführung," K. Rahner, *Praxis des Glaubens* (Freiburg: Herder, 1982) 13.

14. Michael Fahey, "The Decade after the Council," *TS* 38 (1977) 762.

15. "The Church as the Subject of the Sending of the Spirit," *TI* 7, 188.

16. Ulrich Möbs, *Das kirchliche Amt bei Karl Rahner* (Paderborn: Schöningh, 1992) 288; on individual sacraments, see Harvey Egan, *Karl Rahner. Mystic of Everyday Life* (New York: Crossroad, 1998) 162–70.

17. *The Church and the Sacraments,* 22f. Used rarely for Jesus or for a sacrament, the word "symbol" was qualified as a "real-symbol," and Rahner imbued it more with reality than symbolism, seeing that symbol poorly expresses incarnation or sacramentality.

18. "The Presence of the Lord in the Christian Community at Worship," *TI* 10, 83.

19. *KRD* 236; see Mary Hines, *The Transformation of Dogma. Karl Rahner and Dogma* (Mahwah, NJ: Paulist Press, 1989); "Karl Rahner on Development of Doctrine. How Relevant Is Rahner Today?" *Philosophy & Theology* 12 (2000) 111–30.

20. Michael Skelley, *The Liturgy of the World: Karl Rahner's Theology of Worship* (Collegeville: Liturgical Press, 1991) 143.

21. Egan, *Karl Rahner, Mystic of Everyday Life,* 170.

22. *HPT* 1, 142f. Answering Rahner's critics that his writings on the church are not historical enough is Möbs, 89–99.

23. What about preaching, the verbal counterpart to sacrament? From 1953 to 1958 Rahner preached on most Sundays and feasts: *Biblical Homilies* (New York: Herder and Herder, 1966) and *The Great Church Year. The Best of Karl Rahner's Homilies, Sermons, and Meditations* (New York: Crossroad, 1993); see Harvey Egan, "Karl Rahner—Preacher of the Good News," *Karl Rahner. Mystic of Everyday Life* (New York: Crossroad, 1998) 105–29; Thomas O'Meara, "The Priest Preaching in a World of Grace," in D. Dietrich and M. Himes, eds., *The Roman Catholic Priest in the 21st Century* (Franklin: Rowman and Littlefield, 2006). "I think that the function of theology in the life of the church lies in the service that it can and must perform for the church's mission to preach the Gospel of Jesus Christ in the present age. This function has two aspects: theology must help the preacher preach the gospel in such a way that it can really be understood and assimilated today; and theology also has a critical function in preventing the church . . . from becoming a ghetto or a sect within the contemporary world" (*KRD* 50). Here, too, Rahner's distinction between the things of religion and the broader horizons of kingdom and faith is unavoidable. One goal of Christianity is to move people's attention from religious things to what lies beneath, the reign of God, to see that religious things, rites, and creeds must be grounded in something deeper, something holy and healthy. A sermon can aid this deeper dynamic by learning from Jesus' way of teaching; he meets various people—state bureaucrats, religious leaders,

116 God in the World: A Guide to Karl Rahner's Theology

soldiers, foreigners, the sick—searching for identity amid the competing atmospheres of sin and grace. The hearer learns to think more maturely about a divine presence that is intimately present but elusive of control and isolation, the Spirit. The parables of Jesus, experts tell us, are not about new information or changes in rituals and sacral objects resulting from a shift from an old to a new covenant but about the deepest issues in religion; those foundational issues present the relationship of God to us and a theology of how God sees us and wishes to be understood by us. Preaching does not come to its hearers as if they were blank pages upon which some doctrinal ideas or moral suggestions are to be written. A sermon unfolds against the background of the profound messages of the great parables and within the horizon of the rich, if simple, complexity of Jesus' introduction of the kingdom of God. "What the preacher says is a proclamation, a kergyma, not primarily nor ultimately a doctrine. He is handing on a message. His word, insofar as it is his word, is a signpost pointing to the word spoken by another. He must be submerged and unseen behind the message he delivers" ("The People of God in History," *The Content of Faith*, 421). The preacher may preach on concrete topics but he or she does not lose sight of imagining the horizons, the worlds in which the congregation lives. Through preaching, grace and faith touch people.

24. Skelley, *The Liturgy of the World*, 157.

25. "On the Theology of Worship," *TI* 19, 149; see "Considerations on the Active Role of the Person in the Sacramental Event," *TI* 14, 169; *Rahner, The Church and the Sacraments* (London: Burns and Oates, 1974) 76–117.

26. "How to Receive a Sacrament and Mean It," *Theology Digest* 19 (1971) 231.

27. Dych, "Karl Rahner's Theology of Eucharist," *Philosophy & Theology* 11 (1998) 142; see Rahner, "The Prayer of the Individual and the Liturgy of the Church," *Grace in Freedom* (New York: Herder and Herder, 1969) 137–81; *Meditations on the Sacraments* (New York: Seabury, 1977).

28. Paul M. Zulehner, *"Denn Du kommst unserem Tun mit Deiner Gnade zuvor . . ." Zur Theologie der Seelsorge heute. Paul M. Zulehner im Gespräch mit Karl Rahner* (Düsseldorf: Patmos, 1984) 82.

29. Rahner, *Church and World*, 355; "One must consider the study of Rahner's ecclesiology as essentially belonging to a study of his sacramental theology of ministerial office. The two are closely linked and intertwined with each other." Jerry T. Farmer, *Ministry in Community. Rahner's Vision of Ministry* (Louvain: Peeters, 1993) 25.

30. "Notes on the Lay Apostolate," *TI* 2, 319–52; see "The Sacramental Basis for the Role of the Layman in the Church," *TI* 8, 51–74; "The Position of Women in the New Situation in Which the Church Finds Herself," *TI* 8, 75–93. For a basic theology of church ministry and life from the 1960s, see *Theology of Pastoral Action* (New York: Herder and Herder, 1968), a translation of opening sections of *HPT*.

31. "The Church's Limits," *The Christian of the Future* (Freiburg: Herder, 1967) 76.

32. "The New Image of the Church," *TI* 10, 28.

33. "Observations on the Charismatic in the Church," *TI* 12, 88.

34. "On the Theology of Revolution," *TI* 14, 324f.

35. *Selbstvollzug der Kirche, Sämtliche Werke* 19 (Freiburg: Herder, 1995) 83. The following chapter treats his views on participation and church structure.

36. Fahey, "Presidential Address: 1904–1984, Karl Rahner, Theologian," 96.

37. *The Shape of the Church to Come,* 56.

38. "The Role of the Layman in the Church," *TI* 8 (New York: Herder and Herder, 1971) 52–4.

39. "Die Theologie der Erneuerung des Diakonats," *Diaconia in Christo* (Freiburg: Herder, 1962) 285–324; at times Rahner saw the diaconate as a kind of seminal potentiality holding other ministries. "Through this functionalization for and toward the life of the church in its own process his dogmatic ecclesiology opened for the times more and more aspects of that greater fullness that is Christianity" (Schmolly, *Eschatologische Hoffnung in Geschichte,* 342).

40. "Pastoral-Theological Observations on the Episcopacy in the Teaching of Vatican II," *TI* 6, 363; "Vatican II and the Diaconate," *TI* 10, 227ff.

41. Möbs, 247. The implicit ordination is the call, the preparation, the success, the effort of the person under the ecclesial influence of the Spirit. These implicit ordinations may also have an explicit role in commissioning of services (see W. Haunerland, "The Heirs of the Clergy? The New Pastoral Ministries and the Reform of the Minor Orders," *Worship* 75 [2001] 305–20).

42. "Der theologische Ansatzpunkt für die Bestimmung des Wesens des Amtspriestertums," *Concilium* 5 (1969) 196; on the theology of the priest, see Farmer, 173–94; Richard Lennan, *The Ecclesiology of Karl Rahner* (Oxford: Oxford University Press, 1995) 68–74; Thomas O'Meara, "Karl Rahner on Priest, Parish, and Deacon," *Worship* 40 (1966) 103–10.

43. "Reflection on the Concept of Jus Divinum in Catholic Thought," *TI* 5, 226–40.

44. *The Shape of the Church to Come,* 57.

45. "Pastoral Ministries and Community Leadership," *TI* 19, 80; Möbs has drawn together the observations of Rahner and other German theologians on the leaders of parishes who are not presbyters (*Das kirchliche Amt bei Karl Rahner,* 218–34).

46. "Neue Ämter und Dienste in der Kirche," *Praxis des Glaubens,* 296–8.

47. "Meaning of Ecclesiastical Office," *Servants of the Lord* (New York: Herder and Herder, 1968) 21ff. At times Rahner's theology of expanding ministry is a theology of the self-sharing of the divine Persons active in the collective person (Farmer, 207ff.).

48. Farmer, 207; "Consecration in the Life and Reflection of the Church," *TI* 19, 57ff.

49. "The Position of Women in the New Situation in Which the Church Finds Herself," *TI* 8, 75–93; H. van der Meer, *Priestertum der Frau* (Freiburg: Herder, 1969).

50. "Notes on the Lay Apostolate," *TI* 2, 321.

51. "Priestertum der Frau?" *Stimmen der Zeit* 195 (1977) 294.

52. *FW* 163; see Farmer, "Women and Priesthood," *Ministry in Community,* 191–4.

53. "The Pope and the Bishops," *Inquiries* (New York: Herder and Herder, 1964); "The hierarchy is not an aristocracy for the church" ("On the Structure of the People of the Church Today" *TI* 12, 221).

54. "The Teaching Office of the Church," *TI* 12, 11.

55. Ibid., *TI* 12, 8, 9f.

56. "Pastoral-Theological Observations on the Episcopacy in the Teaching of Vatican II," *TI* 6, 362. It is false to conceive of the church as "an absolute monarchy or totalitarian system in which in principle the only measures having any force in the dimension of the social are those decreed, ordained, or at least approved in a positive manner by him who stands at the supreme point of this system . . . , preserved from making any erroneous decision in any essential or decisive matters by the assistance of the Holy Spirit" ("Observations on the Factor of the Charismatic in the Church," *TI* 12, 89); on freedom, church, and the Holy Spirit, see *Meditations on Freedom and the Spirit* (New York: Seabury, 1978).

57. "Basic Theological Interpretation of the Second Vatican Council," *TI* 20, 89.

58. "The New Image of the Church," *TI* 10, 11. "To the extent that humanity really accepts this absolute self-sharing of God offered in an eschatologically irrevocable way in Christ through his grace, sharing that acceptance and making present historically the confessing proclamation of this self-sharing and the sacramental cult of this eschatological event; in social unity human beings are the church" (*HPT* 1, 119).

59. "Observations on the Factor of the Charismatic in the Church," *TI* 12, 81.

60. *HPT* 1, 179–91.

61. "Pastoral-Theological Observations on the Episcopacy in the Teaching of Vatican II," *TI* 6, 361–8; "On Bishops' Conferences," *TI* 6, 369–89; on the election of bishops and other pastoral aspects of the episcopacy see various interviews in *KRD* 23ff., 197ff., 204ff., 321ff., 330ff.

62. *The Dynamic Element in the Church* (New York: Herder and Herder, 1964) 82f.

63. "[A] very good pastoral-theological principle for every bishop and pastor would be: Don't worry about the people who still participate in Catholic life. Rather, go out and convert the people who have good will but also have the impression that the Christianity they've been offered does not make them happy. Convert them" (*IR* 109).

64. *F* 381.

65. "The Teaching Office of the Church in the Present-day Crisis of Authority," *TI* 125; on the nuances between authority and leadership and authority and teaching, see "Authority," *TI* 23, 61–85.

66. "The only way, therefore, in which the theologian can actively engage in theology is for him to be prepared again and again to incur the risk of involuntarily finding the Church against him in his interpretations. If he is unwilling to incur this risk, and confines himself simply to repeating the formulations of the Christian faith put forward by the Church's teaching authority or in other traditional formulae in order to achieve safety in his work, then he runs the (greater) risk of uttering formulae which he only imagines that he has understood" ("Reflections on Methodology in Theology," *TI* 11, 83; see "Intellectual Honesty and Christian Faith," *TI* 7, 67f.).

67. "The Teaching Office of the Church," *TI* 12, 11.

68. Möbs, 30.

69. *FW* 161f. "How boring, old and worn out, conscious only of the appearance of externals, how short-sighted, how desirous of dominance the 'office-holders' in the church seem at times to me. How in a bad sense conservative and clerical" (*Prayers for a Lifetime* [New York: Crossroad, 1984] 115).

70. "Democracy in the Church?," *Grace in Freedom* (New York: Herder and Herder, 1969) 167f. Opposing criticism and opposing change always go together. Criticism and opposition are part of human life in all its dimensions. Offering a new or differing opinion is not critique from outside but from within, not destructive but constructive. To be a critic is to be someone with a strong faith, a lover of the church, and a commitment to pastoral value. In fact, critical and alternative viewpoints are necessary to the church making decisions ("Opposition in the Church" *TI* 17, 127f.; see "The Church's Limits. Against Clerical Triumphalists and Lay Defeatists," *The Christian of the Future*, 49–76; "The Situation of the Society of Jesus since Its Difficulties with the Vatican," *TI* 23, 89–108; "Service without Power," in "Ignatius of Loyola Speaks to a Modern Jesuit," *Ignatius of Loyola* [New York: Collins, 1979] 21–5).

71. Lehmann, *Praxis des Glaubens*, 13; see Roman Siebenrock, "Der Ruf des Konzils in die Reform und die Theologie Karl Rahners," *Theologische-Praktische Quartalschrift* 145 (1997) 123–31.

72. "Structural Change in the Church of the Future," *TI* 20, 131; on the difference between medieval and Baroque ecclesiologies, where church offices are static natures with rights, and a contemporary ecclesiology of activity (131–3).

73. Schmolly, *Eschatologische Hoffnung in Geschichte*, 342.

74. *The Church after the Council* (Freiburg: Herder and Herder, 1966) 31.

75. Lehmann, "Karl Rahner und die Kirche," *VGG* 120–35; see Michael Sievernich, "Karl Rahners Neuinterpretation der Mission," *Zeitschrift für Missionswissenschaft und Religionswissenschaft*, 88 (2004) 158–73.

76. *Content of Faith*, 396.

77. "Aspects of European Theology," *ST* 21, 102f.

78. *The Church after the Council*, 30; see the still valuable programs of *The Shape of the Church to Come* and *The Christian of the Future*.

Chapter 7

The Future
of the World

The dynamics of Karl Rahner's theology—God's loving plan (or plans), salvation history, the expansion of history and church—reach into the future. A salvation history of grace and revelation, the incarnation of the Logos, and the resurrection are particular events within a vast universe of matter, pointing not to an isolated planet of struggle and sin but to a cosmos of intelligence and grace. Incarnation and resurrection touch the material universe and its future.

Christianity proclaims not a past pageant but a stream leading forward. What happened in Jesus, God's union with a human being, continues. As process and evolution penetrated the culture of the twentieth century, the Jesuit theologian showed how the incarnation of the Word in Jesus of Nazareth occurring at one point in time need not fear the long expanses of time behind Bethlehem and ahead of Calvary. History is always becoming future; life ceaselessly points to future life.

I. THE FUTURE OF CHRISTIANITY

To ponder the future of Christianity is not to look at precise questions about the future, like the date of the end of the world, but at the future of humanity comprehended as God's future. Men and women have drawn on God's saving love for thousands, hundreds of thousands of years. Billions of people find in history and culture God's revelatory grace in new variations. As the grace of Christ is everywhere at work, Christianity appears not as one religion among others but as a source and fulfillment. The church is not a small community of salvation but the voice, community, and symbol for the human family.

Is Christianity one religion replacing and fulfilling a second earlier one? Is it one of the world religions denouncing the others, the successor to Judaism or an alternative to Islam and Hinduism? Jesus first preaches the kingdom of God. "Christianity is not an indoctrination into certain conditions or facts or realities which are always the same, but is the proclamation of a history of salvation, of God's salvific and revelatory activity on men and with men."[1] Jesus' metaphors for the kingdom—leaven, renewal, seed, festival—make the Gospel and the church forces within human life and not a kind of ecclesiastical bank or hospital. The Word and the Spirit are the saving force touching all humanity, and this influence does not just begin when a few individuals from the great masses of humanity who have never known Christ enter into baptism.

God's presence is infinitely different from and yet not separate from history on earth. Forward movement, a potential for more—these fashion revelation. "'Direction' is to be understood not as adventitious and coming from without, but rather as the immanent power of this divine self-communication."[2] The future of Christianity comes not from without, not from an angry, even violent God or from scenarios of science fiction but from the realities of history and people within divine life. "But the history of the transcendental revelation of God will necessarily show itself again and again to be a history which is taking place in an irreversible direction towards a highest and comprehensive self-interpretation of man."[3]

II. THE FUTURE OF THE CHURCH

As we saw in the preceding chapter, Vatican II and the postconciliar years have begun to liberate the church, to open it again for its future.

> It's self-evident that only in recent decades has the church moved from being a European Church (which had, of course, the potential for universality) to becoming a genuine world-church. God intended Christianity to be for all people, but until recently it was in fact a European religion which was massively exported to the rest of the world . . . with the help of European colonialism. . . . This world-church now has to promote a greater pluralism among its local churches.[4]

Rahner wrote many essays on forms of the church in their historical context. Although church history seems long, how much of that history brought anything new? When one looks at the categorical forms in church, has the church changed much? One of Rahner's last essays looked imaginatively at the present moment initiating change in light of the history of Christianity. Far from seeing the church as owning a long and varied tradition, one might conclude that the history of the church is just beginning. The church, in its first decades, offered a variety of structures and theologies as it pursued its mission to peoples in the Roman Empire. Then in the second and third centuries it moved beyond being a cluster of groups to being a diverse and dynamic community within Semitic and Hellenic cultures. After that, however, as centuries passed, it remained the same: a Roman organization with Hellenistic thought-forms to which Celtic and Germanic devotions and feudal forms were added. When it existed elsewhere—in the Americas, Asia, Africa—it brought a European synthesis.

> Theologically speaking, there are three great epochs in Church history of which the third has only just begun. . . . First, the short period of Jewish Christianity, and second, the period of the Church in a distinct cultural region, namely that of Hellenism and of European culture and civilization. Third, the period in which the sphere of the church's life is in fact the entire world. These three periods signify three essential and different basic situations for Christianity and its preaching.[5]

Vatican II marks a shift to the international: "that event of church history in which the church modestly began to act precisely as the church."[6] There is "a theological break" in church history. The present time can scarcely be compared to anything in the past except the transition from Jewish to Gentile Christianity. As cultures emerge around the globe, time is bringing newness to the church. "It is incontestable that at Vatican II the church appeared for the first time as a world church in a fully official way."[7] The church is opening to and entering into the entire world. Johann Baptist Metz has accepted Rahner's division of three ages, seeing today to be a time of polycentrism of theologies and church forms, of "the safety of risk," of a positive but limited role for European—Roman political structures and Greek theologies—perspectives so long dominant.[8]

Christianity is moving out from being European (the pontificate of John Paul II shows how easily institutions fall back into being something largely European and premodern). Rahner's theology of the church mirrored the course of his life, moving from theory to practical topics (it also remained partly an ecclesiology of a north European church struggling to see other churches and to address the effects of secularization). His pastoral theology of the church had its sources in the dynamics of trinitarian grace, a healthy existentialism open to growth, and the ordinariness of Ignatian spirituality.[9] For the church of the future, Rahner employed some of his favorite words: task, mission, commission, realization. Structural changes are necessary, for the Spirit cannot flourish amid dictatorship, repression, arrogance, or withdrawal. Basic communities, dynamic parishes, and regional gatherings are the source of the future church. Spiritualities and charisms are a mysticism of the ordinary, while clericalism and fascism can only fade. The intent of Jesus, the teaching of Jesus, the contemporary presence and plan of the Spirit—these are sovereign. "Rahner's numerous publications on ecclesiology—spanning a period of fifty years—called on the church to be open to change in its doctrines, structures, in its relationship with the world."[10]

The inspiration, teaching, and grace of the Spirit come through the members of the Body of Christ, and there is no reason to think, in light of theology or history, that such inspiration is limited to a few hundred bishops. Leadership is to be attentive—more so than ever in this age of education and media—to how the largest number of faithful can share in the decisions of the church. Though written forty years ago, Rahner's observations on the participation of all the baptized and all those active in the ministry in the direction of the church is still valuable. The church's organic life bestowed by universal baptism in the Spirit is a foundation for sharing decision-making. No one political form or ethos determines the constitution of the church. Officeholders have been and are chosen by elections (the pope by cardinals, a bishop by canons): the only difficulty is that there is a too-narrow group of electors. The functional roles in offices should not be an alternative to the role of the people. Dogmatic decisions should not be made by majority vote, but, too, all appointments and decisions should not be made in the manner of an aristocratic totalitarianism. Authority begins with the commissioning words of Jesus on service and evangelization, implying that ministry and life exist within the redeemed people and do not come from sublime, external figures.

Rahner did not see "democracy" as a bad word, an impossible reality for the church. "[Democracy is] that form of society which grants its members the greatest possible freedom and participation in its life and decisions, in accordance with their intellectual, cultural and social condition."[11] A few conceive of the church "as an absolute monarchy or totalitarian system in which in principle the only measures having any force in the dimension of the social are those decreed, ordained, or at least approved in a positive manner by him who stands at the supreme point within this system."[12] The church, however, is a society. Contrary to what feudal clericalism or Baroque administration holds, members have freedom and dignity. The graced activities in which the Spirit of Christ moves through the entire Body are not parceled out by the leadership in minimal amounts. "Democracy wants all the members of a society to cooperate freely in its activities and decisions, and this is easier in a society [with participation and voice] than in one where the individual no longer knows where responsibility lies and feels himself merely as a cog in a machine."[13] What separates the church from democracy is not that Jesus gave it a different political structure, e.g., Roman imperialism or Baroque monarchy, but that the church flows from and follows the divine in a complex interplay of community and action.

The future life of the church must take into account the cultural contours of the age and the ideals of the human person. It cannot advocate the absence of freedom, intellectual stagnation, and administrative obtuseness that were characteristic of the past. If there is a unity in dogma and faith, there is a variety in theology. Church leaders should admit that they have in new areas a lack of information and expertise. The more church leadership furthers open discussion, the less it will appear as a controlling aristocracy, ignorant and imprudent. Criticism, discussion, decision-making in the church is normal, for otherwise there could be no thinking, change, or progress. Every Christian is a human person, and each has his or her ideas and perspectives, some assisted by the Spirit. The Christian is called by faith itself to be in a dialogue with the church and with the Spirit.

> A church that functions in this [authoritarian] approach as the old-fashioned companion of a secular and emancipated society is uninteresting and historically dead. People who, ultimately for personal, psychological reasons, remain in this kind of church and want it to be a humanitarian organization or a swindle cultivating and resembling secular social power, would be better to follow their views outside the church.[14]

The church is not suited to be a museum or a sect.

In Europe, in the late 1970s, Rahner began to speak of a "wintry time" in the church, a retreat away from the energy of Vatican II, a move back into a ghetto, a decoration of the church as a sect or a Baroque shrine. Papal nostalgia and episcopal inertia frustrated the renewal of the church as Vatican bureaucrats discouraged discussion about pastoral problems and possibilities.

> Certainly, it would be foolish and naïve to maintain that the church will suddenly cease to be the tired pilgrim in time, the church of sinners, of the weak and wretched. . . . All renewal, all progress of the church will at the same time be expended in the experience of the laborious course

of history, in the disappointment with ourselves who are still the church. We are always called to play the unfinished symphony of the honor of God but what we achieve is merely a rehearsal.[15]

III. GOD AND INTELLIGENT CREATURES BEYOND EARTH

Questions about the future of Christianity, projects for the church in a long future, reflections on the future of religions and cultures on earth—today these topics lead to an even further horizon. Is there life on other planets, on planets now being discovered with some frequency? If so, what is the role of grace and Jesus Christ in extraterrestrial worlds?

Already in 1964, Rahner had published an encyclopedia article treating "star-dwellers." After mentioning their great distance from us, he noted that the issue has little to do with our personal existence and history. Such creatures cannot be defined "by where they are located in the cosmos," for "their intellectual subjectivity determines that space-time reality."[16] As long as the geocentric image of the world had some validity for the daily experience of the Christian, the cosmos was a visible universe locating human existence in a brief salvation history; the cosmos was a limited place for the salvation history of humans.

> Nowadays the Christian has to live on a tiny planet in a solar system which in its turn is part of a galaxy of a hundred thousand light years with thirty billion stars and this galaxy is estimated to be only one among billions of such galaxies in the universe. . . . What people believe about themselves, their destiny and their worth will not turn out to be deceptive because of their vulnerability in this vast cosmos (theological reasons are still at least as significant as those of modern physics).[17]

To presume that all intelligent creatures in the universe, other than ourselves, are living a life apart from grace and sin "does not do justice to the real and total relationship of God-spirit-grace."[18] It is up to science to pursue the facts, but theology should, given the enormous number of stars, retain an open view toward multiple salvation histories. A Christianity of a God of love and generosity will offer not fear but encouragement in this direction. Why would matter and life reach a point of intelligence open to the gift of grace but go no further? Theologians will not be able to say much on this question and will point to the fact that the purpose of Christian revelation is the salvation of humankind, and not to answer questions that really have no important bearing on the realization of this salvation in freedom.[19]

The Jesuit theologian argued that an extension of graced life into the cosmos cannot be easily dismissed. And yet, the ancient religious view of the cosmos was never empty and monoform, for there were angels, pure spirits. Moreover, one should not presume that other intelligent forms of life exist in a natural sphere outside grace. An advocate of an interplay of grace and human nature would ascribe to creatures of finite spirit a supernatural destiny immediately bestowed by and directed to God. Of course, the gratuitousness of God's offer of a deeper life and the unknown modes of existence and freedom in these creatures remain. Other kinds of knowing and loving creatures in countless planetary societies manifesting the life of God would form a cosmos of grace hardly imaginable. The possibility of intelligent and free life beyond our solar system is the new frontier, certainly for thinking about revelation if not for actual physical exploration.[20]

IV. THE ABSOLUTE FUTURE

To return to earth, the future appears as lengthy as the past, and so the future of grace is long. For each person, the future sooner or later encounters a serious alteration, a change, death. There is the believer's passage from life to death. The Christian faith looks at life after death as a realm continuing life on earth, and yet it is a life obviously but mysteriously different, only glimpsed and believed in. "Eschatology," theology about ultimate realities, is not information about a paradise nor special information about the life of the soul after death but the extrapolation of grace active now in our lives into an unknown future form of life. Salvation history extends beyond death. In Christian eschatology "we know about the present situation of human beings in the history of salvation. We do not project something from the future into the present, but rather in the human experience of himself and of God in grace and in Christ we project our Christian present into the future."[21] A theology of the future is a theology of today.

Biblical images about heaven and hell are pictorial and metaphorical. They tell little about the future. Jesus' preaching, to suit his times, has a few negative images of the future, but remarks about burning in a garbage dump are highly metaphorical. There are also a few phrases in a language of threats.

> Eschatological statements (like those about heaven and hell) are basically statements about humans existing now insofar as they face two possibilities about their future. In this sense the message of Christianity as the radical interpretation of the subjective experience of freedom is absolutely and deadly serious. It says to each one of us—not to someone else—to me personally: in and through yourself, in and through what

you in your innermost depths are and definitively want to be, you can be a person who closes himself into the absolute, deadly and final loneliness of saying "No" to God.[22]

The Gospel does not teach that there are two human lives, one graced and one evil, and two destinies, heaven and hell. Sin and the fulfillment of sin are not an option but a distortion, a road with no exit. Evil decisions and acts deform a good creature fashioned by love, and grace is always silently inviting the most determined sinner to leave a road that goes nowhere and to rejoin the one journey into God. A radical and free rejection of God, hell on earth and beyond, "is one of freedom's possibilities, but this possibility of freedom is always at the same time something abortive, something which miscarries and fails, something which is self-destructive and self-contradictory."[23] A life is a transcendental and existential orientation to God. Life as a personal totality of choices and events has fashioned a dynamic leading to or away from Love. "I believe that in life taken as a whole and at some particular specially blessed moments a decision is reached about one's own life."[24]

The Christian understanding of the future is only in its beginnings. Human beings, in their knowledge and love, are inescapably directed toward this distant and elusive mystery. In revelation and grace, this distant mystery has bestowed itself on humanity as nearness and accessibility.[25] Rahner noted that the twentieth century was composing little Christian theology on death or life after death, and he creatively circled around some aspects of it. What is said about life in the kingdom of God, about grace in each human person, is the beginning and the ground of whatever we would say about "heaven" and "hell." Life beyond death is a future that is absolute: it does not lead to further basic alterations and stages and is not made up of unexpected miracles or stories resembling science fiction. Artists delight in showing how the human spirit seeks life, how it seeks more life and seeks life fulfilled. Human self-transcendence aspiring to love and to know more points to future life; human existence refuses to succumb to the threats of meaninglessness and non-being. Rahner's early exploration of human spirit existing in a world and the varied meanings of incarnation led him to an eschatology that saw grace to be a force affirming the value of matter. The absolute future has already begun: shared divine life is the seed of all future life.

The absolute future begins with death. Death is an event to which life has been tending. If death comes from sin (as the Bible narrates), death also comes from the winding down of our biological life: human existence is weak and fragile. Death is not an accident but a multilayered event in the life of an individual; death sums up a life; it is a stage in life, a passage to further life. This handing on of one's self to God is also a receiving of love and knowledge about life.

> The whole Christian life consists in weaving together realities for whose structuring one can offer no formula that is really practical. When you are young, perhaps you think that you have a grand, maybe even an ideal, theory into which everything fits. But in time, to a certain extent, such an ideological view of life vanishes. And nothing remains for you but to hand over to the eternal God your actions, your disappointments, your sins, your successes—your whole life. Only God can make sense out of this mess. . . . The one incomprehensible mystery of God is a reality and you die into it. At the same time you have in Jesus . . . the promise that this leap into God's incomprehensibility has really succeeded.[26]

Does death set an end to human life? One gives up everything, one lets everything go. And in this emptiness God arrives. Are there further stages of life after death? Christians have thought there might be an intermediate state between death and the eschaton. Is this a time of change, of purgation, of waiting? Past simplistic views of suffering do not make up a dogma and are open to questions and different views. Imagining an intermediate passage, a purgatorial time comes from the Middle Ages and finds a high point in the early twentieth century. Christian faith professes first and foremost the resurrection of the individual person and a deeper life with God. Picturesque views of the next life (waiting, changing) have a basic problem: they are based on a view of time as time exists on earth and upon a reduction of the person to the soul, a spiritual remnant.

When people die, although they have in the plan of God an eternal life, they are morally and spiritually incomplete. Rahner affirmed a time of purification and growth even as he questioned the popular images describing this reality. What arrives is not a time of punishment but of development, because our sins, our weakness and meanness during life remain as an inertia, a resistance against entering communion with God. In a sense, the sinner creates his or her own purgatory—God does not punish those being drawn more deeply into his love—and the sinner sees with wisdom and patience that within her are layers of erratic ambitions and festering resentments.

Does a process of growth take time—in a world where time has faded away? Perhaps death and purgatory are the same. Rahner offered an original perspective on a period of purification.

> Why could not the "duration" of the event of purification be identified with the diverse depth and intensity of the pain that man experiences in

death itself, since there is a terrible difference between what he actually is and what he ought to be? Why should this pain (which is concretely identical with the individual character of dying proper to each person in accordance with his state) not itself be the purifying event which is supposed to constitute the essence of purgatory?[27]

Does the interim state, the line of existence between death and resurrection occur in a few instants rather than in millennia? Certainly it does not take place in time and is not part of the long future history of earth. "Why should we not put the resurrection at that particular moment when the person's history of freedom is finally consummated, which is to say, at death?"[28] Perhaps the resurrection into a future without time takes place not after millennia of earthly time but when the person first enters the eschaton (where time and history no longer exist). Regardless, the self-centered person, immature in faith and in love only with herself, encounters a God whose love is for a while instructive and elevating. Grace for a life becomes more explicit, explaining the past, directing toward the future.

The death of Jesus Christ interprets every death. Baptism is the beginning of death (rising from the water) because it is the beginning of resurrection. Grace given by baptism is capable of overcoming death.[29] Belief in bodily resurrection and eternal life with God is a Christian faith-conviction. Rahner inevitably began his presentation of the resurrection by stating that this central teaching must not be given up no matter how difficult it is for some modern persons to believe it. Why live morally or seriously if life simply ends in a meaningless emptiness? Resurrection, however, is not resuscitation: it is not the reunion of the body with its soul but the fulfillment of this particular person on earth, material and spiritual. Here theology can draw on modern theories and philosophies of the person where existence, temporality, and corporeality receive a new richness from a person's resurrection. Through death the entire human person enters a new existence and a new world, a new corporeal existence. Human beings find resurrection in matter and cosmos, and so it follows that human beings, called by society and church to flee a rigid individualism, have a responsibility for material creation and are drawn to sacramental worship.[30] The more deeply a person enters into God, the more deeply he or she enters into the life of other human beings and into God's one creation. The union of my human reality with God and (in intense love) with others brings no loss or absorption of individuality, for the closer one approaches to God, the more his individuality is liberated and expanded. A further world does not replace but fuels the hope of a better world empowering the courageous struggle for a better economic and social future and warning against exploiting and ruining this world. The future is not utopia after a veil of tears but an empowerment for what is good and human. History will endure, and, on the other hand, it will be radically transformed. This tension gives openness to the future and an importance to the present.

Life now and life after death is individual and social: a person rises as a member of the human family, a family now fully the Body of Christ. There is a "relationship between the fulfillment of an individual person through death, a fulfillment which is going on now continually, and the fulfillment of the human race and with it the *fulfillment of the world*."[31] This future milieu is not the church (no longer needed) but something broader. The person rises into a society of grace triumphant. The human person rises as corporeal spirit and graced creature and so enters not into a heaven of souls but a universe of various creatures. Transcending religious and social differences, grace illumines billions who have discovered God's loving plan vibrating to the ultimate degree within them and their stories. The fulfillment of the whole history of the human family continues on endlessly, a process fired by its irreversible climax in Christ. The resurrection is not a transformation into an angelic life, long and ultimately boring, but a transformation into human society.

Ahead—all religions project and ponder this—lie judgment, heaven, and hell.

For the Christian, there are not two equal paths leading to two places: heaven and hell. Evil is a dead end, a static perversion. The key issue for the person who has radically chosen evil is change: the absence of any positive change in a life of hatred would hold one in that perverse orientation. Can a negative decision last into the next life? Can an elected orientation take on an eternal duration? God has created us to share his life, he loves us, and Christ died for us—those realities permeate existence. To say "No" to them—although possible—is much more difficult than to say "Yes" with one's entire being. "The Christian message says nothing about whether in some people or in many people evil has become an absolute reality defining the *final end and result* of their lives."[32] One might hope that hell is empty.

> I do not say that I could state in the form of an apodictic judgment coming out of my own self-understanding or out of a certain concept of God that "hell" may be empty. One can hope, however, that radically forgiving love can ultimately bring it about that all human beings say a final yes to God so that actually no person must be damned in the face of divine judgment. So I may hope.[33]

Heaven is not a pleasant geographical location but a state of existence, a metamorphosis of human life into a richer life. Heaven is the intensification of the salvation history, of grace, of the self-sharing of God. Jesus is the source of incarnational life for all people. "And the experience of Christ's resurrection is precisely the beginning (not the interruption) of that single process which began long ago, has become irreversible, and now goes on in the saving history of individuals and nations."[34] Even if we cannot imagine eternal life, hope moves us toward it. The Good News of Jesus Christ promises the everlasting and good God as my future.

> If there is such a thing as eternal life at all, if it is not merely something different added to our temporal life and just stretching out over more time, if it is truly the final stage of this present life of freedom which fittingly comes to a final and definitive consummation, only then can we see the unfathomable depths and richness of our existence, of that existence which often gives the impression of consisting of nothing but banalities . . . , something infinitely precious in our life, something able to fill out an eternity.[35]

Men and women live and are changed in the power of God.

Rahner's interpretation of statements in the Bible about the future has influenced many, showing that eschatology, rather than being a collection of curiosities, prophecies already fulfilled, or bizarre prognoses not to be taken literally (but prized by fundamentalists), is a theology of a human future. The reality of the Incarnation impels the trajectory of God's saving history, the missions of Word and Spirit forward. For Peter Phan, Rahner's originality here lies not in a detailed description of dramatic future events at the end of the world but in "a reflection on what God's creative power has brought about in humanity and in the world, and in a 'projection' of this achievement into its mode of final fulfillment on the basis of what has occurred in Jesus Christ."[36] For the fulfillment and transformation of the earth's cosmic milieu, the problem of time in any interim state, and the nature of a transforming stage prior to heaven, he has offered new ideas. Phan lists other creative areas:

> His interpretation of death as a personal act, of death as the consequence of sin, of the death of Christ as a redemptive act precisely as death; his opinion regarding the intermediate state as a cultural amalgam; his justification of purgatory on the basis of the multileveled ontology of the human being and his explication of purgation as integration and transformation; his emphasis on the permanent significance of Christ's humanity for heavenly blessedness; his understanding of hell as a serious possibility for human freedom; his development of a transcendental

hope for the resurrection as the condition of possibility for the belief in Jesus' resurrection and the general resurrection of the flesh; a rapprochement between the doctrine of the resurrection of the body and that of the immorality of the soul; and, finally, his diversification of Christian transcendental consummation from secular, inner-worldly utopias.[37]

In all these insights the principles of Rahner's theology remain active: the human person and her society and church exist in time and culture; the self-sharing of God enters happily into the course of the planet Earth. The difficulties of an individual life and the struggles of a society are places where the future Mystery is already present.

NOTES

1. *F* 138.

2. *F* 156

3. *F* 154.

4. *KRD* 235.

5. "Towards a Fundamental Theological Interpretation of Vatican II," *TI* 18, 721.

6. Ibid., 716. "The church has now more than ever the duty to expose with determination the basic heart of the Christian gospel. And the church must absolutely protect itself from a watered-down humanism wherever it may appear in any form or other. But theologians must make clear through their lives that they really believe and realize that they are dealing with the absolute reality of God who is near and who wishes to communicate himself. This radical nature of the proper, specific Christian gospel cannot be hidden. If that were sufficiently present in a lively way, then many clerical, bureaucratic, and canonical measures would seem totally superfluous" (*FW* [New York: Crossroad, 1990] 200).

7. "Towards a Fundamental Theological Interpretation of Vatican II," 718.

8. On Rahner, Metz, and others treating this analysis of the church leaving a European format, see Mario Delgado, "Perspektiven 'Europäischer Theologie' im Anschluss an Karl Rahner," *TEG* 233–66.

9. See *KRD* 293ff.

10 Richard Lennan, *The Ecclesiology of Karl Rahner* (Oxford: Oxford University Press, 1995) 8.

11. "Democracy in the Church?," *Grace in Freedom* (New York: Herder and Herder, 1969) 150. Rahner expected that in the future the Bishop of Rome would coordinate church decisions reflecting large participation and consensus ("The Teaching Office of the Church in the Present-Day Crisis of Authority," *TI* 12, 3–30).

12. "Observations on the Charismatic in the Church," *TI* 12, 89.

13. "Democracy in the Church?," 155.

14. "Opposition in the Church," *TI* 17, 127.

15. *The Church after the Council* (Freiburg: Herder and Herder, 1966) 29–30. Leo O'Donovan writes: "Admiring courage, he was himself courageous, as a person and as a theologian. Trying quietly to mediate a reconciliation between Hans Küng

and the Vatican, he bore with being treated, as he told me, *'wie ein Hofnarr'* (like a court jester). Furious that his friend Johannes Baptist Metz was denied a chair at the University of Munich after it had been offered to him, he wrote his stinging *'Ich protestiere!'* in the Catholic weekly newspaper *Publik Forum*. Often at the synod of the German bishops in Würzburg, he rose to plead for a greater openness and democratic spirit in the church" ("Losing Oneself and Finding God. Karl Rahner [1904–1984]," *America* 191 [2004] 12). He liked to remark: "You have to fight back" (cited in K.-H. Neufeld, *Die Brüder Rahner* [Freiburg: Herder, 2004] 339).

16. "Sternenbewohner. Theologisch," *Lexikon für Theologie und Kirche* 9 (Freiburg: Herder, 1964) 1061–2; see Thomas F. O'Meara, "Christian Theology and Extraterrestrial Intelligent Life," *TS* 60 (1999) 3–22.

17. "Natural Science and Reasonable Faith," *TI* 21, 49f.

18. "Sternenbewohner. Theologisch," 1062. Rahner's following words—"God-spirit-grace in which grace is always the grace of Christ"—are not an uncritical affirmation of a cosmic centrality of Jesus Christ but a reaction against the advocates in the first half of this century of hypothetical humans of pure nature apart from grace, for instance, prior to Adam and Eve, or of modern people living through a neutral existence in members of the world religions.

19. "In our context it is especially worthy of note that the point at which God in a final self-communication irrevocably and definitively lays hold on the totality of the reality created by him is characterized not as spirit but as flesh. It is this which authorizes the Christian to integrate the history of salvation into the history of the cosmos, even when myriad questions remain unanswered, as can happen" ("Natural Science and Reasonable Faith," *TI* 21, 55).

20. "We must still ask ourselves whether it is not moral vulgarity of a low order to pour out so many billions to send people to the moon, while at the same time we are faced with worldwide hunger" (*KRD* 27).

21. *F* 432.

22. *F* 103–4; "Hell," *SM* 3, 7–9.

23. *F* 102; see *F* 436 and "Eschatologie," *Lexikon für Theologie und Kirche* 3 (Freiburg: Herder, 1959) 1095. Harvey Egan observes that this theology does not support the traditional piety of deathbed conversions: it questions "that the moment of medical death brings with it a special light or grace which allows one to turn one's entire life upside down" (*Karl Rahner. Mystic of Everyday Life* [New York: Crossroad, 1998] 195).

24. *KRD* 246.

25. For Rahner's basic theology amid other approaches in the twentieth century, see Peter Phan, "Introduction," and "Karl Rahner's Eschatology in Context," *Eternity in Time. A Study of Karl Rahner's Eschatology* (Cranbury, NJ: Associated University Presses, 1988).

26. *FW* 105, 106.

27. "Purgatory," *TI* 19, 186.

28. "The Intermediate State," *TI* 17, 120. Rahner discussed a form of reincarnation as a possibility for infants who had had no real life and freedom (Phan, 128–30); see support for Rahner's theory of the intermediate state from theologians and church officials in Phan, 131ff.

29. See *On the Theology of Death* (New York: Herder and Herder, 1965).

30. See P. Michael Petty, *A Faith that Loves the Earth: the Ecological Theology of Karl Rahner* (Lanham, MD: University Press of America, 1996). Philip Geister, *Aufhebung zur Eigentlichkeit. Zur Problematik kosmologischer Eschatologie in der Theologie Karl Rahners* (Uppsala, Sweden: Uppsala University Press, 1996); Michael Skelley, *The Liturgy of the World: Karl Rahner's Theology of Worship* (Collegeville: Liturgical Press, 1991).

31. *F* 446.

32. *F* 103.

33. *FW* 114. The inner obduracy of an eternal hell renders not only a relationship with God but any purpose to human life meaningless. Egan sees hell as a "metaphysical schizophrenia." The love of God, Christ, and the saints is eternal. Does Rahner's theology imply that there would be no purpose to existence without the possibility of grace, to duration without sharing in the divine plan? The cessation of the supernatural existential is the frustration of the matrix of all existentials. God does not create to punish or to leave empty. There is no point for an ungraced nature to live on in a world of grace.

34. "Parousia," *TD* 336.

35. "Eternity from Time," *TI* 19, 177; see "The Theological Problems Entailed in the Idea of the 'New Earth,'" *TI* 10, 270; see "Immanent and Transcendent Consummation of the World," *TI* 10, 273–6.

36. Phan, 202.

37. Ibid., 204.

Conclusion

Years pass and times change. Karl Rahner remained creative, whether offering new insights into structures of the church or sketching a theology of world religions. He spoke more of "today" and less of "the recent past."[1]

The divine self-sharing, grace, could no longer be depicted as a commodity to be acquired or as an extrinsic force to be summoned up by laws, and a believer was less and less a passive figure attending church services, someone needing external controls and internal religious badges. In each person, faith and liturgy, prayer and religious experience, make present Someone seeking to be known. God's salvific will elevates the life and actions of all men and women. This is "the first and the last of God's real plans for the real world."[2]

In areas of Catholic Christian theology, a new model has appeared, owing something to Rahner (and to others). It replaces the model of the single, downward line separating the "haves" from the "have-nots," the chosen from the rejected, the elite from the masses, the sacred from the secular. No one can any longer make sense out of society and church by means of the old delineations and exclusions: Christian and non-Christian, Catholic and non-Catholic, clergy and laity, sacramental and profane. Those too severe divisions fade before the approach of Jesus who leads religious words and things to their source and ground, the kingdom of God. The model of a strict dividing line yields to one of concentric circles. One can describe the center of the circles absolutely or relatively: it can be God, the Holy Spirit, Jesus, or, to a much less degree, a ministerial leader or a sacrament. In the church, Jesus' Spirit is at the center of circles of sacramentality around which baptism and the Eucharist flow first, and then come the other sacraments, followed by countless rituals and devotions. Moreover, the Spirit is the life-principle of the baptized, a center surrounded by circles of people and ministries, some of ordination, some of baptism, some lasting, some temporary. Finally, in the world of religions,

Christianity sees itself as the center of circles where other religions have their message and sacrament, forgiveness and sin.

The basic distinction between the universal presence of God and religious phrases and rituals in peoples' lives and societies leads to this model of the circles. A theology of circles points to the deep presence in grace swirling around every man and woman.[3]

* * *

The preceding chapters of this guide show Rahner to be an eminently Catholic thinker of sacramentality, a postconciliar theologian of change and renewal, a late modern theologian of attention to the individual living amid traditions, and a global theologian of the dialectic of the future Christ and human religions. As recent studies on him illustrate, his thought speaks to psychologies of all sorts, to the ecology of earth and the expanse of cosmos, and to the dialogue of religions.

Clearly, this theology is the opposite of every smug sectarianism, of every fundamentalism of things, of every desire to replace the Gospel with a restoration of Baroque antiquities, of every reduction of faith and theology to acceptable phrases and sparse catechisms. That openness to people and cultures may render this kind of theology suspect to some Protestants and to Catholic reactionaries because it is a guide to believing in a large world and to ministering in a vital church. "The new is always uncomfortable and frightening. We may want through 'new knowledge' only to confirm ourselves. Real truths, however, when they penetrate in a new way into us, frighten us, affect us, threaten us, change us, force us into realms of the spirit in which we cannot confuse normalcy with new insight, in which we don't feel at home."[4]

* * *

It has often been remarked that there is little serious critique of Rahner's theology. One can question whether his understanding of Kant or appropriation of Maréchal is accurate in epistemological details. The emphasis upon knowing and existing, central to the first third of the twentieth century, could only leave less developed the social side of theology. He agreed that his theology did not focus on the Cross of Jesus and sin, although it did not neglect them (no theology can choose as its leitmotifs all the Christian faith). Rahner's theology is inclusive, and so criticism is usually expressing a fear or a lack of emphasis.

Rahner's theory of grace in human history and religion developed a tradition of Catholic theologies reaching back through texts on implicit faith and baptism by orientation to thinkers like Francisco de Vitoria and Thomas Aquinas and further back to Clement of Alexandria. Far from being a novel appreciation of billions of people, his theology of wider grace and implicit faith does not go far beyond positions of the thirteenth century.

* * *

Walter Kasper asks:

> What remains? What lies ahead? Was Rahner only a theologian of tran-
> sition who had an audience as long as there was a need to break up the
> Pian conformity? Did he stand back, afraid of the last consequences of his
> historical understanding of dogma? Did he cling to a dogmatic system
> that renders him the last great neo-scholastic? Or, is Rahner's theology
> surrounded by a great misunderstanding whose fatal consequences he
> himself, firmly anchored in Catholic tradition and full of genius, could
> always hold off but which in his less ecclesially socialized and less genial
> disciples brings forth negative results, results that need a correction?[5]

Both sides are wrong.

> Rahner, precisely because of the dialectical structure in the ground of
> his thought is a classic of Catholic theology. He is a successful case of a
> theology of objective tradition and subjective interpretation, of inherited
> substance and of explosive power. His thinking of genius has a catalytic
> spark . . . , and [his theology] is an exemplary appearance of Catholic
> theology in general. Rahner—for theology as well as for thinking—is
> representative of this age, and he will influence the themes and issues in
> Catholic theology for a long time.[6]

Karl Lehmann writes similarly:

> The path goes further. We need Karl Rahner still. His work—one person
> can hardly grasp it—could be taken from us, because some younger people
> do not understand its presuppositions and some older people neglect the
> memory of the past and seek fads. Rahner is an Atlas who bore the heavy
> burden of fashioning a theology that was responsible and original. He did
> this for all Christians and he did it by exercising all of his human existence,
> striving toward the limits of what is possible for human beings.[7]

Karl Rahner and the future? His themes are still central: the dialogue of grace and personality does not pass away, and concrete issues like the complexity of an individual's life in grace, the world religions, church authority, and ministry are in their beginnings. Lehmann concluded:

> He stands today in the church and society, a vital figure. If one—obviously
> from a certain distance—reads him anew, he seems to be often closer to

our present time than to his earlier period. In terms of the church's situation today many of the writings of Karl Rahner, from all decades, hold prophetic, even visionary elements which can offer a helpful contemporary orientation.[8]

He stood totally in the church but taught salvation for the many outside the church; he had a high respect for the teaching ministry of the church but demanded and advocated the freely expressed opinion of each individual Catholic and a wide process by which teaching is formulated.

Rahner—a realist, an activist, a theologian of history, a mystic of global life, a guide to the future—draws forward and unites. Inspired by him, the church's thinking in the future will be less the theology of a central administration or a European monasticism and more theologies of the churches and of a world-church. Through motifs like seminal realities given by Jesus, historical forms, personal growth, and religious dialogue, Rahner is still bringing together the Spirit of Jesus Christ and the spirit of people in their worlds.

NOTES

1. See Yves Tourenne, *La Théologie du dernier Rahner* (Paris: Cerf, 1995) 31–54.

2. "Concerning the Relationship between Nature and Grace," *TI* 1, 310.

3. Rahner, "Alltagsmystik," *Praxis des Glaubens. Geistliches Lesebuch* (Freiburg: Herder, 1982) 113; see Harvey D. Egan, *Karl Rahner. Mystic of Everyday Life* (New York: Crossroad, 1998) ch. 7.

4. Rahner, "I Believe in the Church," *TI* 7, 103.

5. Kasper, "Karl Rahner—Theologe in einer Zeit des Umbruchs," *Theologische Quartalschrift* 159 (1979) 264.

6. Ibid.

7. Lehmann, "Karl Rahner und die Kirche," *VGG* 134.

8. Lehmann, "Karl Rahner zum Gedächtnis," *Stimmen der Zeit* 212 (1994) 148.

Appendix I

Chronology of Karl Rahner's Life

March 5, 1904	Born in Freiburg im Breisgau, Germany
1922	Enters Society of Jesus at Feldkirch (Austria)
1924–1927	Studied philosophy at Feldkirch and Pullach (Munich)
1927–1929	Jesuit regency teaching Latin at Feldkirch
1929–1933	Studied theology at Valkenburg, The Netherlands
July 26, 1932	Ordained priest by Michel Cardinal Faulhaber at St. Michael's Church, Munich
1934–1936	Doctoral studies in philosophy at Freiburg
1936	Receives doctorate in theology from the University of Innsbruck
1937–1939	Professor of theology at University of Innsbruck
1939–1944	Works in continuing education and pastoral work at a pastoral institute in Vienna
1939, 1941	Publishes *Geist in Welt* and *Hörer des Wortes*
1945–1948	Teaching theology at Pullach
1948–1964	Professor of theology at University of Innsbruck
1954	Publishes first volume of *Theological Investigations*
1961	Named by John XXIII and Cardinal König of Vienna as adviser for the Ecumenical Council, Vatican II
1964–1967	Professor of Christian World-View and the Philosophy of Religion, University of Munich
1967–1971	Professor of Theology, University of Münster, Germany
1971–1981	Lives in Munich
1976	Publishes *Foundations of Christian Faith*
1981	Lives in Innsbruck
March 30, 1984	Dies in Innsbruck

Bibliographical Guides

A first bibliography of Karl Rahner's writings was Georg Muschalek and Franz Mayr, "Karl Rahner. Verzeichnis sämtlicher Schriften, 1924–1964," in *Gott in Welt* 2 (Freiburg: Herder, 1964). That was followed by R. Bleistein et al., *Bibliographie Karl Rahner* 1924–1979 in *Wagnis Theologie* and continued up to the year of his death in 1984 in *Glaube im Prozess* where the number of entries stood at around four thousand; see also Andrew Tallon, "In Dialog with Karl Rahner. Bibliography of Books, Articles and Selected Reviews," *Theology Digest* 26 (1978) 365–85. Bibliographies of writings treating Rahner can be found on the website at the University of Freiburg im Breisgau (Albert Raffelt). The journal at Marquette University, *Philosophy & Theology* brings bibliographical information in its issues devoted to Rahner.

A good path to a first acquaintance with Rahner and his theology is through his interviews such as *I Remember* and *Karl Rahner in Dialogue.*

Rahner's thought is first to be found in the many essays in the volumes of *Theological Investigations.* Daniel T. Pekarske has produced a volume of abstractions of all the essays in the twenty-three volumes of *Theological Investigations* (*Philosophy & Theology* 14 [2002]). Each essay is located in its volume and summarized; references are given to previous drafts and publications. These volumes of essays—both in the German original and English translation—are available in CD-ROM format. Christopher Pedley, "A Bibliographical Aid to Karl Rahner," *The Heythrop Journal* 25 (1983) 319–65 arranges the writings according to important theological topics.

In terms of Rahner's synthetic and mature summary, *Foundations of Christian Faith,* Mark Fischer has published an abridged version as an accessible English paraphrase of the *Foundations of Christian Faith* with introduction and indices: *The Foundations of Karl Rahner* (New York: Crossroad, 2005). A guide through this work is provided by the essays in Leo O'Donovan, ed., *A World of Grace* (New York: Seabury, 1980; Washington: Georgetown University Press, 1995). A second presentation of Rahner's thinking is a systematic compendium by Karl Lehmann and Albert Raffelt, *The Content of Faith. The Best of Karl Rahner's Theological Writings* (New York: Crossroad, 1992).

For access to electronic materials around the world, see the website of the Karl Rahner Society that meets yearly in conjunction with the Catholic Theological Society of America.

Index

Style, Karl Rahner's, 14
Suarez, Francisco, 32

T

Tallon, Andrew, 36, 52, 140
Tarzan, 93
Teaching Ministry in the Church,
110ff., 112f., 118, 123
Teilhard de Chardin, Pierre, 32, 91
Theological Investigations, 4, 18, 30
Theology, 10ff.
Tillich, Paul, 21
Tilliette, Xavier, 91
Time (*see* "History")
Tourenne, Yves, 34, 135, 138
Tracy, David, 52
Transcendental philosophy and
theology, 40ff., 93, 98, 104
Translations of Karl Rahner's
writings, 3

U

University of Munich, 4–8
Urs von Balthasar, Hans, 31, 34, 92

V

Vatican II, Ecumenical Council, 2,
19f., 31, 97, 112, 114, 121, 124
Vitoria, Francisco de, 136
Vorgrimler, Herbert, 2, 3, 15, 19, 62,
92, 114

W

Weigel, Gustave, 21
Welte, Bernhard, 21, 27
Wittgenstein, Ludwig, 13
Women, their roles in the church,
107, 116f.
Worship in the world, 100f.